# EAGLE MOUNTAIN

### INTERNATIONAL CHURCH

# 50 DAYS OF PROSPERITY

## *Volume 1*

## by Pastor George Pearsons

*"He will spend his days in prosperity and*
*his descendants will inherit the land."*
*Psalm 25:13, NIV*

Unless otherwise noted, all scripture is from the *King James Version* of the Bible.

For more information about Kenneth Copeland Ministries, visit kcm.org or call 1-800-600-7395 (U.S. only) or +1-817-852-6000.

ISBN 978-1-60463-141-8
#30-0820

# EAGLE MOUNTAIN
## INTERNATIONAL CHURCH

## DAYS OF PROSPERITY
### Pastor George Pearsons

## Table of Contents

Dear Prosperous Believer,

There is no question whatsoever that it is God's perfect will for us to prosper.

By the time he wrote 3 John 2, the Apostle John was called "The Elder." He had become a wise, mature and respected leader in the Church. His integrity was unquestioned. His humility was unparalleled. And his face-to-face relationship with Jesus on the island of Patmos was astounding, to say the least.

That is why this verse is so significant. One listens very closely to a man of great experience, stature and honor in the Body of Christ. Ask me how I know.

"Beloved, I wish above all things that thou mayest prosper and be in health, even as thy soul prospereth." Notice he said "above all things." To see others prosper and be in health was John's overwhelming passion—a passion that came from the Father. Psalm 35:27 says, "Let the Lord be magnified, which hath pleasure in the prosperity of his servant." We also read in Deuteronomy 8:18, "But thou shalt remember the Lord thy God: for it is he that giveth thee power to get wealth, that he may establish his covenant which he sware unto thy fathers, as it is this day." Philippians 4:19 in *The Amplified Bible* tells us that "my God will liberally supply (fill to the full) your every need according to His riches in glory in Christ Jesus."

Seeing people prosper is also the passion of Kenneth Copeland Ministries.

I began working for KCM in 1976. I became a student of the solid biblical principles of faith that this ministry teaches. I am quite familiar with its mission, having traveled with Kenneth and Gloria Copeland and by listening to countless messages on cassette tapes and then CDs.

From time to time, Brother Copeland would share with congregations what this ministry is called to do. I would write down what he would say and keep a collection of those "mission statements." One day, he spoke about his calling where prosperity was concerned.

He said, "This ministry is called to teach the laws that govern prosperity and supernatural increase and abundance." I could hear the deep sense of responsibility in his voice. I received that mandate as my own, both as a believer in Christ Jesus and as the pastor of Eagle Mountain International Church.

With that said, you can clearly understand the purpose of this *50 Days of Prosperity* study series.

The beginning of this series began when Gloria asked me to teach two weeks on the *Believer's Voice of Victory* broadcast. At the time, I was teaching a prosperity series in church. It was no surprise when the Lord spoke up in my spirit and told me to teach a television series titled, *10 Days of Prosperity.*

He went on to say, *As much as I want My people healed, I want them to prosper financially and provisionally. I want My people to thrive and flourish in these times. I want them to experience My supernatural provision. Lack and poverty are under the curse. Tell them that they are redeemed from the curse and that they are to walk in the fullness of THE BLESSING. My people are not subject to the times, no matter what is happening around them. Totally immerse them in the Word of prosperity. By doing this, the Word will build their faith and enlarge their capacity to believe and receive. Now, get with the program!* It was a very strong word!

The Lord impressed me to prepare the outlines in advance and make them available to the television audience. I taped the first 10 programs by myself.

Several weeks after the broadcasts aired, I received one of the most significant phone calls of my life. It was Gloria Copeland calling. "George," she said, "I have had a brilliant idea. I just watched your broadcasts and I want you and me to do the next prosperity series. There is one stipulation—I want you to bring your notes!"

I heartily accepted the offer. Those notes have not been difficult to prepare. I have been taught by the very best! The reference materials are endless. And, what an amazing time we have had. I have learned so much more by taping with Gloria. It is obvious that the message of prosperity is deep within her spirit. I must say that teaching with Gloria has been one of the greatest highlights of my life. What an honor!

I happened to mention something to Gloria while taping our first broadcast together. "Gloria, you just can't exhaust the subject of prosperity," I said. She quickly answered and said, "Let's try!!"

Fifty broadcasts later, we decided to assemble this study series.

I encourage you to immerse yourself in your own "50 Days of Prosperity"—or take whatever time necessary to thoroughly study each outline. Perhaps you could study one outline each week. Imagine, "50 Weeks of Prosperity"! You could conduct your own Bible study with friends and family. Pastors and ministers are already using them to preach. Others are referring to them whenever they receive offerings. The possibilities are endless!

All of us at Kenneth Copeland Ministries want you to prosper. But, as we all know, a transformation of the mind takes total immersion in the Word. So, get out your Bibles and notes, and "get with the program!" The results of this series may be found in Psalm 25:13 (NIV): "They will spend their days in prosperity, and their descendants will inherit the land."

Thriving and prospering with you,

Pastor George Pearsons

# EAGLE MOUNTAIN
### INTERNATIONAL CHURCH

## DAYS OF PROSPERITY
### Pastor George Pearsons

## God Wants Us to Prosper

### Day #1

*"He will spend his days in prosperity and his descendants will inherit the land."*
*(Psalm 25:13, NIV)*

A.  3 John 2:
    1.  "Beloved, I wish above all things that thou mayest prosper and be in health, even as thy soul prospereth."
    2.  AMP: "Beloved, I pray that you may prosper in every way…."
B.  Psalm 35:27: "Let them shout for joy, and be glad, that favour my righteous cause: yea, let them say continually, Let the Lord be magnified, which hath pleasure in the prosperity of his servant."
C.  Deuteronomy 8:18: "Thou shalt remember the Lord thy God: for it is He that giveth thee the power to get wealth, that he may establish his covenant which he sware unto thy fathers, as it is this day."
D.  2 Chronicles 16:9: "For the eyes of the Lord run to and fro throughout the whole earth, to show himself strong in the behalf of them whose heart is perfect toward him…."
E.  Proverbs 10:22: "The blessing of the Lord, it maketh rich, and He addeth no sorrow with it."
F.  Philippians 4:19:
    1.  "But my God shall supply all your need according to his riches in glory by Christ Jesus."
    2.  AMP: "And my God will liberally supply (fill to the full) your every need according to His riches in glory in Christ Jesus."
G.  God has a covenant determination to prosper us. Our responsibility is to believe it and receive it.
H.  True prosperity is the ability to use God's power to meet the needs of mankind in every realm of life—spirit, soul, body, financially, emotionally, etc.

# DAYS OF PROSPERITY
**Pastor George Pearsons**

## Not Subject to the Times

### Day #2

**A. We Are Not Subject to the Times**
1. We are not subject to, and do not live under, the dominion, rule, control or influence of whichever way the economy and world system is going at the moment.
2. The times are subject to the authority of the Word, the blood and the Name of Jesus spoken and acted upon by the believer.
3. The times are subject to us.
4. We are subject to and governed by another economy and another system—the kingdom of God.
5. We live in the secret place.
   a. Psalm 27:1-6: "In the time of trouble he shall hide me in his pavilion…."
   b. Psalm 32:6-7: "Thou art my hiding place…."
   c. Psalm 31:14-15: "My times are in thy hand…."

**B. John 17:13-22—We Are Separated From the World's Failing System**
1. We are to thrive and not just survive.
   a. *Survive*—barely get by, merely exist
   b. *Thrive*—flourish, succeed, advance, prosper
2. Verse 14: We are not of this world's system.
3. Verse 15: "…Keep them from the evil."
   a. Matthew 6:13: "Deliver us from evil…."
   b. Galatians 1:4: "…Deliver us from this present evil world."
   c. 1 John 5:18: "…That wicked one toucheth him not."
   d. 1 Corinthians 10:13: He has made a way to escape.
4. Verse 17: Sanctified from the world through the Word
   a. *Sanctified*—Separated and cut away from the effects of
   b. Romans 8:2: "The law of the Spirit of life in Christ Jesus hath made me free [has separated me] from the law of sin and death."
5. We thrive and prosper in tough times.
   a. We are not subject to the economy.
   b. We flourish in spite of what is happening.
   c. Untouched and unaffected

**C. Exodus 8:23—The Wall of Redemption**
1. Verses 20-23: No swarms of flies
2. 9:1-7: Cattle didn't die
3. 9:22-26: No hail
4. 10:21-23: Light in the land
5. Galatians 3:13: Separated from the curse
   a. Verse 9: "They which be of faith are blessed...."

# Word From the Lord
## Given to Kenneth Copeland
## August 6, 2010

## Everything Is Going to Be ALL-RIGHT in the Household of Faith

The world is in *serious* trouble. But for the household of faith and those who will cling to My Word and listen *very* carefully, and do this thing that I have demonstrated before you tonight, and night after night after night. You can do that. You can do it yourself. You can stand in your place and you can worship, and you can praise in the face of hell itself. And you can praise yourself into that place where you say, "Ha, ha, ha. Everything is going to be all right."

The world, I'll tell you again, is in *serious* trouble. Some very hard things are coming, in different places around the world. Very difficult times in a lot of places. They're that way now, but they'll not get better. They will continue to get worse and worse and worse. It is on a downhill run that the world cannot stop. <u>But, for the household of faith, everything's going to be all right.</u> <u>Everything is going to be all right.</u>

Oh, yeah—you'll have to make a stand. You'll have to fight the good fight of faith. But, when did you not have to do that? These are dangerous times. They're dangerous times financially. They're dangerous times in the earth because the earth is weighted under a *gross* weight of sin. There are things and places and situations underneath the earth, in the oceans, in the heavens. Things are being rattled and shaken. The earth is trying to break in different places.

Stand on My Word and it'll not come nigh you. Praise and worship My Name. Don't *feed* and *feed* fear and *feed* trouble into your life and into your mouth. No, no, no, no. Quit living in that house. <u>Get on back over here in the household of faith.</u> Feed on My Word, not on the bread of sorrow. Feed on My Word. Look in My face. Praise and worship. And praise and worship. In church, praise and worship and preach the Word. Praise and worship and preach the Word. Praise and worship and preach the Word. Everything's going to be all right.

For as I have said, and will continue to say until it becomes solid and strong in your spirit—<u>your time has come.</u> It is your time to excel. It is your time to do exceeding, extraordinary things in the financial world, in the medical world, in all of the areas where the world is in such dire trouble and so confused that they're confused beyond their ability to understand how confused they really are. And they're hurting because of it. They are crying out because of it. People are trying to take advantage of people because they're so confused and because they're so troubled.

And I'll tell you right now there are politicians and there are so-called business people and there are thieves and there are all kinds of demonic folks who are trying to take advantage of My people during a confusing time, and I will tell you right now, saith the Lord, you can write it down and you can know it for sure, I won't put up with it and I'll stop them from doing such a thing. And you are going to see some things happen.

Fear not. I have My eye on them. They will go so far and no further. Their end is already determined. I'll not put up with it, saith the Lord of grace. I will not put up with it. They have pushed Me and pushed Me and invited Me out of their lives and their thinking and in many cases and many personalities and many people that are at the forefront of the news in this hour, I have already turned over to a disobedient, reprobate mind.

I am the Lord and I will not have My people run roughshod over, My people who are crying out to Me. I utter My Word through my servant tonight and you make mark of it. But, everything is going to be all right in your house. Hallelujah. Amen.

———————

I never have, until I heard that coming up in my spirit and then I saw it in the spirit, I saw the word *all right,* everything is going to be (spelled) "all-right." All-right.

Glory to God. Anything else, Lord, that You want to deliver? Praise God, Yes, Sir.

Now before you are seated, I want you to say to someone, "I believe that. Everything is going to be all-right." Take hold of it. Take hold of it. Everything is going to be ALL-RIGHT.

# EAGLE MOUNTAIN
### INTERNATIONAL CHURCH

## DAYS OF PROSPERITY
**Pastor George Pearsons**

### Same Conditions—Different Results

#### Day #3

**A. Jeremiah 17:5-8: Same Conditions—Different Results**
1. The cursed man trusts himself; his heart is not toward God.
2. The result: no fruit, no hope, no future
3. The blessed man trusts God with his whole heart.
4. The result: thriving tree, roots deep, no fear, produces fruit
5. Verse 17:8 (MSG): "They're like trees replanted in Eden, putting down roots near the rivers. Never a worry through the hottest of summers, never dropping a leaf. Serene and calm through droughts, bearing fresh fruit every season."

**B. Luke 6:46-49: Same Storm—Different Outcome**

**C. Confession**
I am not moved by what I see.
I am not moved by what I hear.
I am not subject to the times.
I will keep obeying God.
I will keep tithing.
I will keep sowing seed.
I will keep walking by faith.
I will keep going to church.
I am separated from the curse of lack.
I am connected to THE BLESSING of Abraham.
I am thriving, flourishing, increasing, enlarging,
    experiencing God's supernatural provision.
I call September...
    PROSPERITY MONTH for my household.

# Word From the Lord
## Given to Charles Capps
## February 1, 1978

## Financial Inversion Shall Increase In These Days

Financial inversion shall increase in these days. For you see, it is My desire to move in the realm of your financial prosperity. But release Me, saith the Lord, release Me that I may come in your behalf and move on your behalf.

For yes, yes, yes, there shall be in this hour financial distress here and there. The economy shall go up and it will go down; but those that learn to walk in the Word, they shall see the prosperity of the Word come forth in this hour in a way that has not been seen by men in days past.

Yes, there's coming a financial inversion in the world's system. It's been held in reservoirs of wicked men for days on end. But the end is nigh. Those reservoirs shall be tapped and shall be drained into the gospel of Jesus Christ. It shall be done, saith the Lord. It shall be done in the time allotted and so shall it be that the word of the Lord shall come to pass that the wealth of the sinner is laid up for the just.

Predominantly in two ways shall it be done in this hour. Those who have hoarded up and stored because of the inspiration of the evil one and held the money from the gospel shall be converted and drawn into the kingdom. But many, many will not. They'll not heed the voice of the Word of God. They'll turn aside to this and they'll turn to that and they'll walk in their own ways, but their ways will not work in this hour. It'll dwindle and it'll slip away as though it were in bags with holes in them. It'll go here and it'll go there and they'll wonder why it's not working now. "It worked in days past," they'll say.

But it shall be, saith the Lord, that the Word of the Lord shall rise within men—men of God of low esteem in the financial world—that shall claim the Word of God to be their very own and walk in the light of it as it has been set forth in the Word, and give. They'll begin to give small at first because that's all they have, but then it will increase, and through the hundredfold return, so shall it be that the reservoirs that have held the riches in days past, so shall it return to the hands of the giver. Because of the hundredfold return shall the reservoirs be lost from the wicked and turned to the gospel. For it shall be, it shall be in this hour that you will see things that you've never dreamed come to pass. Oh, it'll be strong at first in ways, then it will grow greater and greater until men will be astounded and the world will stand in awe because the ways of men have failed and the ways of God shall come forth.

As men walk in My Word, so shall they walk in the ways of the Lord. Oh yes, there will be some who say, "Yes, but God's ways are higher, surely higher than our ways, and we can't walk in those." It's true that the ways of God are higher. They are higher than your ways as the heavens are above the earth, but I'll teach you to walk in My ways. I never did say you couldn't walk in My ways. Now learn to walk in them. Learn to give. So shall the inversion of the financial system revert and so shall it be that the gospel of the kingdom shall be preached to all the world, and there shall be no lack in the kingdom. Those that give shall walk in the ways of the supernatural! They shall be known abroad. My Word shall spread and the knowledge of the Lord shall fill all the earth in the day and the hour in which ye stand. Ye shall see it and know it, for it is of Me, and it shall come to pass, saith the Lord.

**EAGLE MOUNTAIN**

I N T E R N A T I O N A L   C H U R C H

## DAYS OF PROSPERITY
**Pastor George Pearsons**

### Thriving in the Midst of Famine

#### Day #4

A. **Genesis 26:1—There Was a Famine in the Land**
1. *Famine*
    a. Severe shortage
    b. Extreme scarcity
    c. Serious economic downturn
2. Dark time for those who…
    a. Don't know God
    b. Don't know their covenant with God
    c. Fear, panic, uncertainty, hopelessness
3. What the Word tells *us* about famine
    a. Job 5:20, 22 (NLT): "He will save you from death in time of famine…. You will laugh at destruction and famine."
    b. Psalm 33:18-19: "The eye of the Lord is upon them that fear him, upon them that hope in His mercy [NLT—rely on His unfailing love]; to deliver their soul from death, and to keep them alive in famine."
    c. Psalm 37:18-19: Even in famine they will have more than enough.
        i. HEB: "…He will supply until no more is needed."
4. In famine, we don't just survive—<u>WE</u> <u>THRIVE!</u>
    a. Prosper, flourish, succeed, advance
    b. Grow vigorously
    c. Increase in goods and estate
5. Proverbs 10:22: "The blessing of the Lord, it maketh rich, and he addeth no sorrow with it."

B. **Genesis 26—Isaac Thrived in Famine**
1. Verses 1-6: Stay where you are—*obedience.*
    a. God needed him there
    b. God needs us right here, right now
    c. Zechariah 8:13 (NLT): "Among the other nations, Judah and Israel became symbols of a cursed nation. But no longer! Now, I will rescue you and *make you both a symbol and a source of blessing.* So don't be afraid. Be strong, and get on with rebuilding the temple!"

d.  We are a symbol of THE BLESSING
e.  We are a source of THE BLESSING
    i.  Genesis 12:2-3 (AMP): "I will make of you a great nation, and I will bless you [with abundant increase of favors] and make your name famous and distinguished, and you will be a blessing [dispensing good to others].... In you will all the families and kindred of the earth be blessed [and by you they will bless themselves]."
    ii. Psalm 21:6 (AMP): "...You make him to be blessed and a blessing forever."
2.  Verse 12: He sowed and received *in the same* year one hundredfold—and the Lord blessed him
    a.  *Unusual yield*—even in fertile regions, not greater than twenty-five to fiftyfold
    b.  Psalm 65:11-13 (NLT): "You crown the year with a bountiful harvest; even the hard pathways overflow with abundance. The grasslands of the wilderness become a lush pasture, and the hillsides blossom with joy. The meadows are clothed with flocks of sheep, and the valleys are carpeted with grain. They all shout and sing for joy!"
    c.  In the same year
3.  Verse 13: Isaac waxed great, went forward and became very great
    a.  (NLT): He became a rich man and his wealth only continued to grow.
    b.  He was thriving—flourishing, succeeding, advancing, growing vigorously, increasing in goods, estates, bulk and stature
    c.  He became stronger and more powerful in wealth and influence.
4.  Verse 14: He had possessions of flocks of sheep, herds of cattle and a great store of servants
    a.  Philistines were jealous
    b.  They wanted to stop him
5.  Verses 22-24: He didn't give up—he wouldn't quit
    a.  *Rehobeth* (HEB) = room, streets, a broad and spacious place, an enlargement.
    b.  (NLT): "...At last the Lord has created enough space for us prosper [thrive, flourish, succeed, advance and grow vigorously] in this land."

## C.  In Order to Thrive in Times of Famine, We Must Keep Doing What Isaac Did
1.  Keep obeying God
    a.  Obedience is where THE BLESSING is
    b.  Isaiah 1:19: "If ye be willing and obedient, ye shall eat the good of the land."
2.  Keep sowing seed
    a.  It is always a good time to sow into the kingdom of God
    b.  Ecclesiastes 11:4 (AMP): "He who observes the wind [and waits for all conditions to be favorable] will not sow, and he who regards the clouds will not reap."
3.  Keep tithing
    a.  Isaac tithed—how do we know?
    b.  Genesis 14:20: Abraham gave tithes of all
    c.  Genesis 18:19: "For I know him, that he will command his children and his household after him, and they shall keep the way of the Lord...."

4. Keep on walking by faith
    a. Isaac didn't quit standing in faith
    b. Hebrews 10:35 (AMP): "Do not, therefore, fling away your fearless confidence, for it carries a great and glorious compensation of reward."
    c. Galatians 6:9 (AMP): "Let us not lose heart and grow weary and faint in acting nobly and doing right, for in due and at the appointed season we shall reap, if we do not loosen and relax our courage and faint."
5. Psalm 92:12-14: Keep attending church
    a. Verse 12: "The righteous shall flourish like the palm tree: he shall grow like a cedar in Lebanon."
    b. Verse 13: "Those that be planted in the house of the Lord shall flourish in the courts of our God."
    c. Verse 14: "They shall still bring forth fruit in old age; they shall be fat and flourishing."
        i. Our future is secure in Him

**D. Thriving In a Time of Famine—Confession**
I am not moved by what I see.
I am not moved by what I hear.
I am going up higher.
I am going to keep obeying.
I am going to keep sowing.
I am going to keep believing.
I am going to keep receiving.
I am going to keep on walking by faith.
In a time of famine, we are thriving.
We are prospering.
We are flourishing.
We are succeeding.
We are advancing.
We are growing vigorously.
We are increasing.

**EAGLE MOUNTAIN**

INTERNATIONAL CHURCH

## DAYS OF PROSPERITY
**Pastor George Pearsons**

## Walking in the Fullness of The Blessing

### Day #5

**A. Romans 15:29—The Fullness of The Blessing**
1. (GNB): I shall come with a full measure of The Blessing
2. Fullness = Greek word *pleroma*
3. To be filled up, full, complete, to be fully furnished and liberally supplied
    a. Philippians 4:19 (AMP) "My God will liberally supply (fill to the full) your every need according to His riches in glory in Christ Jesus."
4. To fill to the top so that nothing is wanting; to fill to the brim so that nothing is lacking
    a. Example of a ship fully manned with sailors, rowers and soldiers and fully loaded with supplies, freight and merchandise
5. *Plethora*—overabundance, excessive amount, superabundance

**B. Genesis 1:27-28—A Quick Review of The Blessing**
1. The very first words heard by a human ear, setting the course and precedent for God's perfect will for man
2. Man was empowered by The Blessing in order to:
    a. Be fruitful
    b. Multiply
    c. Replenish the earth
    d. Subdue the earth
    e. Have dominion over the earth
3. The Garden of Eden was a perfect demonstration of God's plan for this planet. It was a prototype of what He wanted the planet to look like. Adam's job was to exercise his God-given authority and expand that Garden until it encompassed the entire earth. That was what The Blessing was for.
4. It provided Adam with the power to carry on the work God began at Creation. It equipped him with the divine resources he needed to follow God's example. He was to transform the uncultivated parts of this planet into a veritable Garden of Eden by speaking faith-filled words. The Blessing empowered Adam to be The Blessing wherever he went. The Garden of Eden was literally inside Adam.

5. Jesus came to restore The Blessing that was lost at the Fall
    a. Jesus is The Blessing—the last Adam.
    b. Jesus—The Blessing—now is alive in us.
    c. We have been redeemed from the curse and now walk in The Blessing of Abraham.

## C. Galatians 3:13-14—Redeemed From the Curse to Walk in The Blessing
1. *Redeem*—to buy back, to buy out, to clear by payment
2. To free a person from captivity by paying a ransom
3. We have been freed from the curse of poverty.
    a. Lack
    b. Deficiency
    c. Not enough
    d. Shortage
4. We are redeemed from "paycheck-to-paycheck," just barely getting along.
5. Proverbs 10:22: "The blessing of the Lord, it maketh rich, and He addeth no sorrow with it."

## D. Deuteronomy 28:1-14—Walking in the Fullness of The Blessing
1. Verse 2: All these blessings shall come on you and overtake you.
    a. Brenton: All these blessings shall come upon you and shall find you
    b. HEB = will reach you
2. Verse 8 (MSG): "God will order a blessing on your barns and workplaces...."
    a. CEV: "The Lord your God is giving you the land, and He will make sure you are successful in everything you do...."
3. Verse 11 (MSG): "God will lavish you with good things...."
    a. AMP: "The Lord shall make you have a surplus of prosperity...."
    b. BBE: "The Lord will make you fertile in every good thing...."
    c. REV: "The Lord will make you abound in prosperity...."
4. Verse 12 (MSG): "God will throw open the doors of His sky vaults and pour rain on your land on schedule and bless the work you take in hand. You will lend to many nations but you yourself won't have to take out a loan."
    a. AMP: "The Lord shall open to you His good treasury...."
    b. NLT: "The Lord will send rain at the proper time from His rich treasury in the heavens and will bless the work you do...."
    c. *Treasury* in the Hebrew = depository, armory
    d. BBE: He will open His storehouse in heaven.
    e. CEP: "The Lord will open the storehouses of the skies."
5. I am walking in the fullness of The Blessing,
    fully furnished and liberally supplied.
Filled to the top—nothing wanting.
Filled to the brim—nothing lacking.
My ship is full and overflowing.
The Blessing has come to me.
The Blessing has overtaken me.
I am walking in the superabundant,
    exceeding excess, fullness of The Blessing.

# EAGLE MOUNTAIN
INTERNATIONAL CHURCH

## DAYS OF PROSPERITY
**Pastor George Pearsons**

## Our Relationship to Money

### Day #6

**A. The Role of Money in Our Lives**
1. Money issues can be a source of stress and pressure
2. They control lives, attitudes and emotions
3. Some are slaves to money—driven to make it and keep it
4. We must straighten out our relationship with money
5. Goal: Financial Attitude Adjustment

**B. Matthew 6:24-33—Settle This: I Serve God. Money Serves Me**
1. Genesis 1:29: Seed was designed by God to serve us
2. Psalm 104:14: Seed is for the service of man
3. Mark 10:17-22: Example of a man serving money
4. Mark 12:41-44: Example of money serving a woman
     a. 2 Corinthians 9:6: This is what she did

**C. 1 Timothy 6:10, 17-19: How We Conduct Ourselves With Money**
1. Verse 10: The love of money is the root of all evil
2. We don't love money—we love God
3. Verse 17: We don't trust money—we trust God
4. Verse 18: We are givers of money—not takers
5. Money is a tool to help others

**D. My Confession of Faith**
I settle this issue right now.
I adjust my financial attitude.

I do not serve money.
I am not a slave to money.
I serve God.
Money serves me.

I do not work for money.
Money works for me.

Money doesn't control me—I control money.
Money doesn't rule me—I rule money.
Money doesn't dominate me—I dominate money.

I fearlessly tithe as I am told.
I boldly give as I am led.
Money—you serve me.
Money—you obey me.
Money—you multiply, increase and produce maximum harvest.

Harvest—I command you to come to me now—in Jesus' Name!

## DAYS OF PROSPERITY
**Pastor George Pearsons**

## Supernatural Provision

### Day #7

**A. Matthew 17:24-27—Money in a Fish's Mouth**

    1. Demonstration of supernatural provision—"Bring it on, birds!" Testimony Tommy Williams shared several years ago how he spoke to the birds to bring him money. Based upon 1 Kings 17, Tommy started finding money around the house after he went out and hollered at the birds.

    A 15-year-old was so impressed with this story that he decided to try it. He asked the Lord for $10 for missions.

    He went out, spoke to the birds and commanded them to put it in a tree in the backyard. The first day he discovered 65 cents, the second day $2.35, and the third day $7. Over the next two months, he found a total of $440 in the tree!

    2. Foreign to natural man's thinking
    3. Unusual, unlimited, accelerated supply from heaven
    4. Supersedes the realm of impossibility
    5. God has supernatural ways to fully supply every need in the face of lack, shortage and a bad economy.
        a. He makes the way when they say there is no way.

**B. What We Must Do to Experience Supernatural Provision**

    1. Enlarge our capacity for supernatural provision
    2. See God supernaturally supplying the need
    3. Feed on the Word
    4. Renew our minds
    5. Exercise our faith

**C. Faith-Building Scriptures for Supernatural Provision**

    1. James 1:17: "Every good gift and every perfect gift [AMP—free, large, full] is from above, and cometh down from the Father of lights, with whom is no variableness, neither shadow of turning.

    2. Ephesians 3:20-21 (AMP): "Now to Him Who, by the [action of His] power that is at work within us, is able to [carry out His purpose and] do superabundantly, far over

and above all that we [dare] ask or think [infinitely beyond our highest prayers, desires, thoughts, hopes or dreams]—to Him be glory in the church...."

3. Philippians 4:19 (AMP): "My God will liberally supply (fill to the full) your every need according to His riches in glory in Christ Jesus."
   a. *Supply* in the Greek—fill up, make full, furnish liberally, fill to the top so that nothing shall be wanting, fill to the brim so that nothing shall be lacking

4. Psalm 68:19: "Blessed be the Lord, who daily loads us with benefits, even the God of our salvation."

5. Isaiah 55:1: "Every one that thirsteth, come to the waters, and he that hath no money; come ye, buy, and eat; yea, come, buy wine and milk without money and without price."

## D. Examples of Supernatural Provision

1. Genesis 22:6-14: God supernaturally provided a ram for the sacrifice.
   a. Verse 14: Abraham called the name of that place, "The Lord will provide."

2. 1 Kings 17:1-6: God supernaturally provided ravens to bring food and drink to Elijah.

3. 1 Kings 17:8-16: God supernaturally provided a one-year supply of food for the widow in the midst of a famine.
   a. Verse 14: The barrel of meal and the bottle of oil would not be empty until the rain returned.
   b. Verse 15: She, he and her house did eat a full year.
   c. Verse 16 (NLT): No matter how much they used, there was always enough left over in the containers.

4. 2 Kings 4:1-7: God supernaturally provided supernatural debt cancellation for the widow.
   a. The woman kept pouring oil from a small pot into as many empty vessels as they could find.

5. 2 Kings 6:1-7: God supernaturally caused a borrowed, lost ax head to float to the surface of the water.

6. John 2:1-11: Jesus supernaturally turned water into wine.
   a. 180 gallons of wine

7. John 6:5-14: Jesus supernaturally multiplies the fish and loaves and feeds 20,000.
   a. Word from the Lord through Brother Copeland, "You are going to be the ones who God uses to supernaturally feed the lost when disasters come. Only, it is not going to be like it was in the past. In many cases, you are not even going to need the trucks and airplanes. In a lot of cases, you are just going to take one little meal and divide it and divide it and divide it."
   b. Jesus touched the loaves and fishes and they supernaturally multiplied.

## E. Galatians 6:7-8—Sowing Is a Supernatural Action

1. "Those who give shall walk in the ways of the supernatural." —Kenneth Copeland
2. When you sow into the kingdom of God, you reap from the kingdom of God.
3. Giving and tithing are supernatural acts.
4. Expect to reap supernatural things.
5. There are many supernatural streams of provision and income available in God's kingdom—believe and receive!

## DAYS OF PROSPERITY
**Pastor George Pearsons**

## Supernatural Debt Cancellation

### Day #8

**A. Luke 4:14-21—Three Ways God Supernaturally Removes Debt**
1. He provides the finances.
2. He removes the debt.
3. He moves upon others.

**B. He Provides the Finances**
1. 2 Kings 4:1-7 (NLT): "…Sell the olive oil and pay your debts, and you and your sons can live on what is left over."
2. Luke 5:1-11: Simon Peter's fishing business avoided bankruptcy after Jesus told him where to drop the nets.
3. Matthew 17:24-27: Taxes were paid from money in a fish's mouth.

**C. He Removes the Debt**
1. Nehemiah 5:1-13: Nehemiah cancelled the debts of the poor Jews.
2. Matthew 18:23-27: The king forgave his servant of the 10,000 talents.
3. Matthew 6:12: Key point—forgive us our debts as we forgive our debtors.
4. Colossians 2:13-14 (AMP): Jesus "cancelled and blotted out and wiped away the handwriting of the note…with its legal decrees and demands. He set it aside and cleared it completely out of our way by nailing it to [His] cross."
5. Luke 16:1-7: He reduces the debt.
    a. EMIC testimony—debt reduced 75 percent (from $6,500 down to $1,600)

**D. He Moves Upon Others**
1. Philemon 18-19 (AMP): "If he has done you any wrong in any way, or owes anything [to you], charge that to my account. I, Paul, write it with my own hand—I promise to pay it in full…."
2. Luke 10:30-37: The Samaritan took out two pence and gave them to the owner of the inn and said to him, "Take care of him. Whatever else you have to spend, I will pay it back in full when I return."

3. God is the One who moves upon a person—not you.
    a. Faith puts no pressure on others.
    b. Faith puts pressure on the Word of the covenant.
    c. Faith says, "God is my source."
    d. Luke 6:38: You give and it will be given to you.

## E. Word From the Lord Through Brother Copeland
1. The manifestation of The Blessing is at an all-time high. You are approaching a "Blessing manifestation of glory" that is an explosion in ways and intensity that the human race has never seen before.
2. The Blessing will surround you. The Blessing will incase you. You will learn to walk in the secret place of the Most High God, blessed in His Blessing, blessed in His glory, blessed in your comings, blessed in your goings and blessed in your pocketbook.
3. All debt will have to get up and leave you the way leprosy left the lepers of old.
4. Debt is financial sickness. It is financial leprosy. It is an attempt to do with the natural world's monies and abilities what I created The Blessing to do for you. Only, it is a burden and not a blessing. Debt is part of the curse.
5. If you will begin to confess the Word, you will be shocked and thrilled at how quickly you will have the glory arise and drive the debt out of your life.
6. If you will bring your tithe to Me and spend time with Me, tithing that tithe to Me, I will teach you and I will train you and I will show you how to be debt free. I will bless you beyond your means. I will bless you beyond your income. I will bless you beyond your salaries. I will bless you beyond anything you have ever known before. I will show you things that you have never heard of before.
7. You will take advantage of those things and be financially blessed. I will bring such a financial blessing upon you that you won't have any idea where it came from. It has come to an explosive place.
8. I am ready, saith the Lord, if you will begin to confess it, walk in it and make it a priority in your life. Then, the glory will manifest in the midst and you will give Me praise. I will come and visit you and together, we will have a grand time.

# EAGLE MOUNTAIN
### INTERNATIONAL CHURCH

## DAYS OF PROSPERITY
**Pastor George Pearsons**

## Making Withdrawals From Our Heavenly Account
### Day #9

**A. Philippians 4:14-19—The Bank of Heaven**
1. There are bank accounts on earth
   a. Philemon 18 (AMP): "If he has done you any wrong in any way or owes anything [to you], charge that to my account."
   b. John 12:6 (AMP): Judas had the "bag, the money box, the purse of the Twelve."
   c. 2 Chronicles 31:11: Hezekiah commanded [the people] to prepare chambers [in the Hebrew, *storehouses*] in the house of the Lord
   d. You can have earthly accounts—just don't put your trust in them.
2. There are bank accounts in heaven
   a. Matthew 6:19-21: They are not subject to theft, ruin, corruption or economic conditions of any kind
   b. Luke 12:33 A treasure in heaven that fails not
3. Many do not realize they already have an account in heaven
4. The Philippians had established an account in heaven
   a. Verse 15 (GOS): "No church but yours went into partnership and opened an account with us."
   b. They opened their account by giving
5. Verse 17 (AMP): Not that I seek or am eager for [your] gift, but I do seek and am eager for the fruit which increases to your credit [the harvest of blessing that is accumulating to your account]."
   a. CON: I seek fruit which accrues to your account
   b. TCNT: I am anxious to see abundant returns placed to your account
   c. MOF: I am anxious for the interest that accumulates to your divine account
   d. NASB: I seek for the profit which increases to your account
   e. NJB: What I value most is the interest that is mounting up in your account

**B. Matthew 6:19-21—Making Deposits**
1. Lay up—make deposits
2. Malachi 3:10: Tithing
3. Mark 10:29-30: Investing in the gospel

4. Proverbs 19:17: Giving to the poor
    a. Matthew 19:21: "Go and sell that thou hast, and give to the poor, and thou shalt have treasure in heaven."
5. 1 Chronicles 16:29: Giving as a praise to God

## C. 1 Timothy 6:17-19—Making Withdrawals

Kenneth and Gloria Copeland were living in Tulsa, Okla. He was a preacher without a place to preach and driving a worn-out car with 95,000 "hard" miles. They had children to take care of and college to pay for. Up until this point, their financial track record was not good at all.

They owed people with no apparent way to ever pay them back.

But after hearing Kenneth E. Hagin preach about faith from Mark 11:23, they decided to take action. They gathered all their debts. They listed every person and the amount owed. They calculated in great detail what it would take for them to operate their household. They included a 15% pad in their budget for extras. They determined what they needed in their immediate future. All of this information was written on paper in a formal prayer of agreement.

Days went by before they would sign their names to the agreement. They prayed and fasted. They repented before God for not being a good representative of the Lord Jesus Christ. They agreed together according to Romans 13:8 that they would never borrow another dime. They committed to God that they would pay back everyone they owed. They continued to make deposits into their heavenly account by faithfully tithing and sowing seed.

They released their faith and made a withdrawal from their heavenly bank account.

This process took time, effort, prayer, focus and diligence. They saturated themselves with God's Word and cut off every voice of the world—no TV or newspapers—just the Word of God.

Praise God—twelve months from that day, every debt was paid in full and every need was completely met.

## D. Seven-Point Bank of Heaven Withdrawal
1. Decide on the amount you need (James 1:5-8)
    a. Be exact and single-minded
    b. Write it down
    c. List your needs, debts and desires
2. Get in agreement with people of like faith (Matthew 18:19-20)
3. Claim what you need by faith (Mark 11:23-24)
4. Bind the devil and his forces (Matthew 18:18)
    a. "Satan, take your hands off my money!"
5. Loose the angels to go get it (Hebrews 1:4)
    a. "Ministering spirits—go get my money!"

6. Continually praise God for it (Psalm 34:1)
7. Avoid strife and unforgiveness (James 3:16; Mark 11:25-26)

## E. Sample Prayer of Agreement

"Father, in the Name of Jesus, we make a withdrawal of $_____ from our heavenly bank account. We have this money in our account and we are withdrawing this amount now. We believe we receive $_____. As in Mark 11:23-24, we believe it in our hearts and confess now that it is ours in the Name of Jesus. We agree that we have this amount according to Matthew 18:19. From this day forward, we roll the care of this over on to You and thank You for it. Satan, we take authority over you; we bind your operation now and render you helpless. Ministering spirits, we charge you to go forth and cause this amount to come to us according to Hebrews 1:14. Father, we praise Your Name for meeting our needs according to Your riches in glory by Christ Jesus, and for multiplying our seed for sowing, in the Name of Jesus."

**EAGLE MOUNTAIN**

INTERNATIONAL CHURCH

## DAYS OF PROSPERITY
**Pastor George Pearsons**

## Call In Your Harvest

### Day #10

**A. Word from Keith Moore to EMIC About Harvesting—9/28/99**
1. Concerning EMIC's giving, God's heart is grieved. It is bothering God that we are not reaping. People are deceived in their thinking if they are just waiting on God to bring it to them.
2. Some are disillusioned and aggravated with God. "How much more can I give?" You think you are waiting on God. You think reaping is automatic. You think once you put the money in, it's all up to Him. You just sit back and relax and think it's all going to just come on you. That is ignorance and confusion.
3. I challenge you to hear the word of the Lord and make up your mind. "I am not just a good giver. I am a good reaper. I am going to get real good at reaping."
4. Proverbs 10: 4-5: "He becometh poor that dealeth with a slack hand: but the hand of the diligent maketh rich. He that gathereth in summer is a wise son: but he that sleepeth in harvest is a son that causeth shame."
5. We can't sleep through our harvest or allow our harvest to stand in the field.

**B. Mark 4:26-29—Harvesting Is Our Responsibility**
1. The man did the sowing, God gave the increase and the man did the reaping.
2. Proverbs 6:6-8: "Go to the ant, thou sluggard; consider her ways, and be wise: which having no guide, overseer, or ruler, provideth her meat in the summer, and gathereth her food in the harvest."
3. Ecclesiastes 11:4: "He that observeth the wind shall not sow; and he that regardeth the clouds shall not reap."
4. Galatians 6:7-9: "Be not deceived; God is not mocked; for whatsoever a man soweth, that shall he also reap. For he that soweth to his flesh shall of the flesh reap corruption; but he that soweth to the Spirit shall of the Spirit reap life everlasting. And let us not be weary in well doing: for in due season we shall reap, if we faint not."
5. Ecclesiastes 3:1-2 (NLT): "For everything there is a season, a time for every activity under heaven. A time to be born and a time to die. A time to plant and a time to harvest."

## C. How to Reap Your Harvest

1. A preacher was struggling financially. Physically, he was well and strong. He had powerful demonstrations of the spirit. The ministry was growing. The only area of trouble was in the financial realm. He took time to fast and pray, seeking the Lord to find out why. The Lord told him that he was not in faith where his finances were concerned. He told him that he had to receive his finances the same way he received his healing—by faith.
2. We call in our harvest by faith
3. Isaiah 41:15: "I will make thee a new sharp threshing instrument having teeth...."
   a. *Teeth* in the Hebrew = mouths
   b. Mouths harvest whatever they speak
4. Our words of faith bring in the harvest
5. Command the angels to go get our harvest
   a. Hebrews 1:14: "Are they not all ministering spirits, sent forth to minister for them who shall be heirs of salvation?"
   b. Matthew 13:39: The reapers are the angels
   c. Psalm 103:20: "Bless the Lord, ye his angels, that excel in strength, that do His commandments, harkening unto the voice of his word."

# EAGLE MOUNTAIN
### INTERNATIONAL CHURCH

## DAYS OF PROSPERITY
**Pastor George Pearsons**

## EMIC Prosperity Confession

We believe we receive....
    Jobs or better jobs
    Raises and bonuses
    Benefits
    Sales and commissions
    Settlements
    Estates and inheritances
    Interest and income
    Rebates and returns
    Checks in the mail
    Gifts and surprises
    Lost money found
    Bills paid off
    Debts demolished
    And royalties received.

This is my year of overflow!
I expect more out of heaven
than ever before.
I receive my harvest
by faith in Jesus' Name.

# DAYS OF PROSPERITY
**Pastor George Pearsons**

## Not Subject to the Times

### Day #11

**A. We Are Not Subject to the Times**
1. We are not subject to, nor do we live under, the dominion, rule, control or influence of whichever way the economy and the world system are going at the moment.
2. Our times are subject to the authority of the Word, the blood and the Name of Jesus spoken and acted upon by the believer
3. The times are subject to us
4. We are subject to and governed by another economy and another system—the kingdom of God
5. We live in the secret place
    a. Psalm 27:1-6: "In the time of trouble he shall hid me in his pavilion…."
    b. Psalm 32:6-7: "Thou art my hiding place…."
    c. Psalm 31:14-15: "My times are in thy hand…."

**B. John 17:13-22—We Are Separated From the World's Failing System**
1. We are to thrive and not just survive
    a. *Survive*—barely get by, merely exist
    b. *Thrive*—flourish, succeed, advance, prosper
2. Verse 14: We are not of this world's system
3. Verse 15: "…Keep them from the evil."
    a. Matthew 6:13: "Deliver us from evil…."
    b. Galatians 1:4: "…Deliver us from this present evil world."
    c. 1 John 5:18: "…That wicked one toucheth him not."
    d. 1 Corinthians 10:13: God has made a way to escape
4. Verse 17: Sanctified from the world through the Word
    a. *Sanctified*—separated and cut away from the effects of
    b. Romans 8:2: "The law of the Spirit of life in Christ Jesus hath made me free [has separated me] from the law of sin and death."
5. We thrive and prosper in tough times
    a. We are not subject to the economy
    b. We flourish in spite of what is happening
    c. Untouched and unaffected

**C. Exodus 8:23—The Wall of Redemption**
1. Verses 20-23: No swarms of flies
2. 9:1-7: Cattle didn't die
3. 9:22-26: No hail
4. 10:21-23: No darkness in the land
5. Galatians 3:13: Separated from the curse
    a. Verse 9: "They which be of faith are blessed…."

**D. Jeremiah 17:5-8—Same Conditions, Different Results**
1. The cursed man trusts himself, his heart is not toward God
2. The result: no fruit, no hope, no future
3. The blessed man trusts God with his whole heart
4. The result: thriving tree, roots deep, no fear, produces fruit
5. Verse 8 (MSG): "They're like trees replanted in Eden, putting down roots near the rivers—never a worry through the hottest of summers, never dropping a leaf, serene and calm through droughts, bearing fresh fruit every season."

**E. Genesis 26:1—Isaac Sowed in Famine and Reaped a Hundredfold**

# EAGLE MOUNTAIN
### INTERNATIONAL CHURCH

## DAYS OF PROSPERITY
**Pastor George Pearsons**

## Flourishing in the Household of Faith
### Day #12

**A. Everything Is Going to Be ALL-RIGHT in the Household of Faith**
*Word from the Lord through Brother Copeland, August 6, 2010*

The world is in *serious* trouble. But for the household of faith and those who will cling to My Word and listen *very* carefully, and do this thing that I have demonstrated before you tonight, and night after night after night. You can do that. You can do it yourself. You can stand in your place and you can worship, and you can praise in the face of hell itself. And you can praise yourself into that place where you say, "Ha, ha, ha. Everything is going to be all right."

The world, I'll tell you again, is in *serious* trouble. Some very hard things are coming, in different places around the world. Very difficult times in a lot of places. They're that way now, but they'll not get better. They will continue to get worse and worse and worse. It is on a downhill run that the world cannot stop. But, for the household of faith, everything's going to be all right. Everything is going to be all right.

Oh yeah—you'll have to make a stand. You'll have to fight the good fight of faith. But, when did you not have to do that? These are dangerous times. They're dangerous times financially. They're dangerous times in the earth because the earth is weighted under a *gross* weight of sin. There are things and places and situations underneath the earth, in the oceans, in the heavens. Things are being rattled and shaken. The earth is trying to break in different places.

Stand on My Word and it'll not come nigh you. Praise and worship My Name. Don't *feed* and *feed* fear and *feed* trouble into your life and into your mouth. No, no, no, no. Quit living in that house. Get on back over here in the household of faith. Feed on My Word, not on the bread of sorrow. Feed on My Word. Look in My face. Praise and worship. And praise and worship. In church, praise and worship and preach the Word. Praise and worship and preach the Word. Praise and worship and preach the Word. Everything's going to be all right.

For as I have said, and will continue to say until it becomes solid and strong in your spirit—your time has come. It is your time to excel. It is your time to do exceeding, extraordinary things in the financial world, in the medical world, in all of the areas where the world is in such dire trouble and so confused that they're confused beyond their ability to understand how confused they really are. And they're hurting because of it. They are crying out because of it.

B. **Psalm 92:12-15:** "The righteous shall flourish like the palm tree: he shall grow like a cedar in Lebanon. Those that be planted in the house of the Lord shall flourish in the courts of our God. They shall still bring forth fruit in old age; they shall be fat and flourishing; to show that the Lord is upright: he is my rock, and there is no unrighteousness in him."
  1. *Flourish* (Hebrew) = to flower, blossom, bloom, break through, spread out
  2. Enter into a state of prosperity
  3. Increase in wealth, favor and honor
  4. Grow vigorously and exuberantly, enlarge and expand
  5. Become extremely successful

C. **Proverbs 14:11:** "The house of the wicked shall be overthrown; but the tabernacle of the upright shall flourish."

D. **Psalm 52:8:** "I am like a green olive tree in the house of God: I trust in the mercy of God for ever and ever."
  1. *Green* (Hebrew) = flourishing

E. **Psalm 112:3:** "Wealth and riches shall be in his house: and his righteousness endureth for ever."

F. **Jeremiah 17:7-8:** "Blessed is the man that trusteth in the Lord, and whose hope the Lord is. For he shall be as a tree planted by the waters, and that spreadeth out her roots by the river, and shall not see when heat cometh, but her leaf shall be green; and shall not be careful in the year of drought, neither shall cease from yielding fruit."
  1. Leaf shall be green—prospering, thriving, flourishing
  2. NLT: "…Their leaves stay green [and flourishing], and they never stop producing fruit."
  3. MSG: "…They're like trees replanted in Eden, putting down roots near the rivers—never a worry through the hottest of summers, never dropping a leaf, serene and calm through droughts, bearing fresh fruit every season."

G. **Psalm 36:7-9 (AMP):** "How precious is Your steadfast love, O God! The children of men take refuge and put their trust under the shadow of Your wings. They relish and feast on the abundance of Your house; and You cause them to drink of the stream of Your pleasures. For with You is the fountain of life; in Your light do we see light."

H. **Song of Solomon 2:4:** "He brought me to the banqueting house, and his banner over me was love."

I. **Proverbs 11:28:** "He that trusteth in his riches shall fall: but the righteous shall flourish as a branch."

# EAGLE MOUNTAIN
### INTERNATIONAL CHURCH

## DAYS OF PROSPERITY
**Pastor George Pearsons**

## Supernatural Wealth Transfer

### Day #13

**A. Financial Inversion Shall Increase in These Days**
*Word from the Lord through Charles Capps, February 1, 1978*

Financial inversion shall increase in these days. For you see, it is My desire to move in the realm of your financial prosperity. But release Me, saith the Lord, release Me that I may come in your behalf and move on your behalf.

For yes, yes, yes, there shall be in this hour financial distress here and there. The economy shall go up and it will go down; but those who learn to walk in the Word, they shall see the prosperity of the Word come forth in this hour in a way that has not been seen by men in days past.

Yes, there's coming a financial inversion in the world's system. It's been held in reservoirs of wicked men for days on end. But the end is nigh. Those reservoirs shall be tapped and shall be drained into the gospel of Jesus Christ. It shall be done, saith the Lord. It shall be done in the time allotted and so shall it be that the Word of the Lord shall come to pass that the wealth of the sinner is laid up for the just.

Predominantly in two ways shall it be done in this hour. Those who have hoarded up and stored because of the inspiration of the evil one and held the money from the gospel shall be converted and drawn into the kingdom. But many, many will not. They'll not heed the voice of the Word of God. They'll turn aside to this and they'll turn to that and they'll walk in their own ways, but their ways will not work in this hour. It'll dwindle and it'll slip away as though it were in bags with holes in them. It'll go here and it'll go there and they'll wonder why it's not working now. "It worked in days past," they'll say.

But it shall be, saith the Lord, that the Word of the Lord shall rise within men—men of God of low esteem in the financial world—who shall claim the Word of God to be their very own and walk in the light of it as it has been set forth in the Word, and give. They'll begin to give small at first because that's all they have, but then it will increase, and through the hundredfold return, so shall it be that the reservoirs that have held the riches in days past, so shall it return to the hands of the giver. Because of the hundredfold return shall the reservoirs be lost from the wicked and turned to the gospel. For it shall be, it shall be in this hour that you will see things that you've never dreamed come to pass. Oh, it'll be strong at first in ways, then it will grow greater and greater until men will be astounded and the world will stand in awe because the ways of men have failed and the ways of God shall come forth.

As men walk in My Word, so shall they walk in the ways of the Lord. Oh yes, there will be some who say, "Yes, but God's ways are higher, surely higher than our ways, and we can't walk in those." It's true that the ways of God are higher. They are higher than your ways as the heavens are above the earth, but I'll teach you to walk in My ways. I never did say you couldn't walk in My ways. Now learn to walk in them. Learn to give. So shall the inversion of the financial system revert and so shall it be that the gospel of the kingdom shall be preached to all the world, and there shall be no lack in the kingdom. Those who give shall walk in the ways of the supernatural! They shall be known abroad. My Word shall spread and the knowledge of the Lord shall fill all the earth in the day and the hour in which ye stand. Ye shall see it and know it, for it is of Me, and it shall come to pass, saith the Lord.

**B. Proverbs 13:22—The Wealth of the Sinner Is Laid Up for the Just**
1. AMP: "…The wealth of the sinner [finds its way eventually] into the hands of the righteous, for whom it was laid up."

**C. Job 27:16-17 (NIV):** "Though he heaps up silver like dust and clothes like piles of clay, what he lays up the righteous will wear, and the innocent will divide his silver."
1. NLT: "Evil people may have piles of money and may store away mounds of clothing. But the righteous will wear that clothing, and the innocent will divide that money."
2. Verse 19 (NLT): "The wicked go to bed rich but wake to find that all their wealth is gone."

**D. Ecclesiastes 2:26 (NIV):** "To the person who pleases him, God gives wisdom, knowledge and happiness, but to the sinner he gives the task of gathering and storing up wealth to hand it over to the one who pleases God…."
1. NLT: "…If a sinner becomes wealthy, God takes the wealth away and gives it to those who please Him."

**E. Proverbs 28:8 (NLT):** "Income from charging high interest rates will end up in the pocket of someone who is kind to the poor."

**F. Psalm 105:37 (AMP):** "He brought [Israel] forth also with silver and gold, and there was not one feeble person among their tribes."
1. *Feeble* (Hebrew) = there was not one pauper among their tribes
2. *Pauper*
   a. An extremely poor person
   b. A person without any means of support
   c. A destitute person who depends on aid from public welfare funds or charity

3. *Tehillim* Commentary
    a. Rabbi Eliezer the Great taught: The lowliest among the children of Israel brought ninety donkeys laden with silver and gold when he left Egypt.
    b. The pauper is a man who has become impoverished and stumbled from his original financial level. No Jew who left Egypt could be described as a pauper because all were enriched by the possessions of their oppressors.
    c. Ibn Yachya and Sforno describe the pauper as a man whose health has deteriorated to the point that he stumbles unless he uses a cane. When the Jews left Egypt, a miracle occurred—not a single person among them was sick or debilitated.

**G. Psalm 105:43 (AMP):** "He brought forth his people with joy, and his chosen ones with gladness and singing."
    1. *Tehillim* Commentary
        a. God did not merely load their saddlebags with material wealth
        b. He filled their hearts with spiritual wealth
        c. The redeemed ones reaped a rich harvest of faith, the outgrowth of the wonders they beheld
        d. This filled their hearts with mirth and their mouths with song

# EAGLE MOUNTAIN
INTERNATIONAL CHURCH

## DAYS OF PROSPERITY
**Pastor George Pearsons**

## Supernatural Increase and Multiplication
### Day #14

A. **Psalm 115:12-16:** "The Lord hath been mindful of us: he will bless us; he will bless the house of Israel; he will bless the house of Aaron. He will bless them that fear the Lord, both small and great. The Lord shall increase you more and more, you and your children. Ye are blessed of the Lord which made heaven and earth. The heaven, even the heavens, are the Lord's: but the earth hath he given to the children of men."

B. **Shall Increase You More and More** (HEB) = Continue to add, over and above

C. **Psalm 67:5-7:** "Let the people praise thee, O God; let all the people praise thee. Then shall the earth yield her increase; and God, even our own God, shall bless us. God shall bless us; and all the ends of the earth shall fear him."
    1.  MSG: "You mark us with blessing, O God…."

D. **Psalm 85:12:** "Yea, the Lord shall give that which is good; and our land shall yield her increase."

E. **Leviticus 26:4:** "Then I will give you rain in due season, and the land shall yield her increase, and the trees of the field shall yield their fruit."
    1.  Leviticus 26:9 (AMP): "For I will be leaning toward you with favor and regard for you, rendering you fruitful, multiplying you, and establishing and ratifying My covenant with you."

F. **Genesis 26:12-14 (NLT):** "When Isaac planted his crops that year, he harvested a hundred times more grain than he planted, for the Lord blessed him. He became a very rich man, and his wealth continued to grow. He acquired so many flocks of sheep and goats, herds of cattle, and servants that the Philistines became jealous of him."

G. **Job 42:12 (NIV):** "The Lord blessed the latter part of Job's life more than the former part. He had fourteen thousand sheep, six thousand camels, a thousand yoke of oxen and a thousand donkeys."

**H. 2 Corinthians 9:10 (NLT):** "For God is the one who provides seed for the farmer and then bread to eat. In the same way, he will provide and increase your resources and then produce a great harvest of generosity in you."

**I. Proverbs 9:11:** "For by me thy days shall be multiplied, and the years of thy life shall be increased."

# EAGLE MOUNTAIN

INTERNATIONAL CHURCH

## DAYS OF PROSPERITY
**Pastor George Pearsons**

## Jehovah Jireh—Our Supernatural Provider

### Day #15

*Our God has unlimited avenues and unusual ways of providing*
*that extend beyond our natural limitations.*

**A. Genesis 22:1-14:** Jehovah Jireh—the Lord will provide
    1. Verse 14: "And Abraham called the name of that place Jehovah-jireh: as it is said to this day, In the mount of the Lord it shall be seen."
    2. Verse 14 (CEV): "Abraham named that place, 'The Lord Will Provide.' And even now people say, 'On the mountain of the Lord it will be provided.'"

**B. Leviticus 26:4-5, 9-10 (AMP):** "I will give you rain in due season, and the land shall yield her increase and the trees of the field yield their fruit. And your threshing [time] shall reach to the vintage and the vintage [time] shall reach to the sowing time, and you shall eat your bread to the full and dwell in your land securely. ...For I will be leaning toward you with favor and regard for you, rendering you fruitful, multiplying you, and establishing and ratifying My covenant with you. And you shall eat the [abundant] old store of produce long kept, and clear out the old [to make room] for the new."
    1. Verse 10 (NLT): "You will have such a surplus of crops that you will need to get rid of the leftovers from the previous year to make room for each new harvest."
    2. Verse 10 (NIV): "You will still be eating last year's harvest when you will have to move it out to make room for the new."

**C. Deuteronomy 28:8, 11-12 (AMP):** "The Lord shall command the blessing upon you in your storehouse and in all that you undertake. And He will bless you in the land which the Lord your God gives you. ...And the Lord shall make you have surplus of prosperity, through the fruit of your body, of your livestock, and of your ground, in the land which the Lord swore to your fathers to give you. The Lord shall open to you His good treasury, the heavens to give the rain of your land in its season and to bless all the work of your hands; and you shall lend to many nations, but you shall not borrow."

**D.** **1 Samuel 2:8 (AMP):** "He raises up the poor out of the dust and lifts up the needy from the ash heap [NLT—garbage dump], to make them sit with nobles and inherit the throne of glory. For the pillars of the earth are the Lord's, and He has set the world upon them."
   1. *The glory of God*—the presence of God heavy with everything good

**E.** **Psalm 23:1, 5 (AMP):** "The Lord is my Shepherd [to feed, guide, and shield me], I shall not lack.… You prepare a table before me in the presence of my enemies. You anoint my head with oil; my [brimming] cup runs over."

**F.** **Psalm 34:10 (AMP):** "The young lions lack food and suffer hunger, but they who seek (inquire of and require) the Lord [by right of their need and on the authority of His Word], none of them shall lack any beneficial thing."

**G.** **Psalm 36:7-9 (AMP):** "How precious is Your steadfast love, O God! The children of men take refuge and put their trust under the shadow of Your wings. They relish and feast on the abundance of Your own house; and You cause them to drink of the stream of Your pleasures. For with You is the fountain of life; in Your light do we see light." (NLT—the light by which we see)

**H.** **Psalm 66:12:** "Thou hast caused men to ride over our heads; we went through fire and through water: but thou broughtest us out into a wealthy place."

**I.** **Psalm 68:19:** "Blessed be the Lord, who daily loadeth us with benefits, even the God of our salvation. Selah."
   1. Psalm 103:2 (AMP): "Bless (affectionately, gratefully praise) the Lord, O my soul: and forget not [one of] all His benefits."

**J.** **Psalm 85:12 (AMP):** "Yes, the Lord will give what is good, and our land will yield its increase."
   1. NLT: "Yes, the Lord pours down His blessings. Our land will yield its bountiful harvest."

**K.** **Psalm 115:14-15:** "The Lord shall increase you more and more, you and your children. Ye are blessed of the Lord which made heaven and earth."

**L.** **Malachi 3:10 (AMP):** "Bring all the tithes (the whole tenth of your income) into the storehouse, that there may be food in My house, and prove Me now by it, says the Lord of hosts, if I will not open the windows of heaven for you and pour you out a blessing, that there shall not be room enough to receive it."

**M.** **2 Corinthians 9:8-12 (AMP):** "And God is able to make all grace (every favor and earthly blessing) come to you in abundance, so that you may always and under all circumstances and whatever the need be self sufficient [possessing enough to require no aid or support and furnished in abundance for every good work and charitable donation]. As it is written, He [the benevolent person] scatters abroad; He gives to the poor; His deeds of justice and goodness and kindness and benevolence will go on and endure forever! And [God] who provides [KJV = ministers] seed for the sower and bread for eating will also provide and multiply your [resources for] sowing and increase the fruits of your righteousness [which manifests itself in active goodness, kindness and charity]. Thus you will be enriched in all things and in every way, so that you can be generous and [your generosity as it is] administered by us will bring forth thanksgiving to God. For the service that the ministering of this fund renders does not only fully supply what is lacking to the saints (God's people), but it also overflows in many [cries of] thanksgiving to God."

N. **Philippians 4:19 (AMP/Greek paraphrase):** My God will liberally supply, fill to the full, cram, furnish, satisfy, finish and complete all of your needs, employment, requirements, lack and business according to His riches, His wealth, His money and His possessions in glory by Christ Jesus.

O. **1 Timothy 6:17 (AMP):** "As for the rich in this world, charge them not to be proud, arrogant and contemptuous of others, nor to set their hopes on uncertain riches, but on God, Who richly and ceaselessly provides us with everything for [our] enjoyment."

P. **2 Peter 1:3:** "…His divine power hath given unto us all things that pertain unto life and godliness, through the knowledge of him that hath called us to glory and virtue."

## DAYS OF PROSPERITY
**Pastor George Pearsons**

## Our Covenant of Wealth

### Day #16

A. **2 Chronicles 16:9:** "For the eyes of the Lord run to and fro throughout the whole earth, to show himself strong in the behalf of them whose heart is perfect toward him."
   1. Show Himself strong (HEB) = bestow, grant, extend His covenant wealth
   2. Our covenant with God is His total commitment to support, defend, protect and provide.
   3. God's consuming passion and determination is to locate His covenant people and bless them.
   4. It is an undying covenant devotion that propels Him to extend Himself to us with everything He is and with everything He has.
   5. It is a covenant love that won't give up or quit until the extension of that love is satisfied.
      a. 2 Samuel 9:1-3: David was consumed with locating an heir of Jonathan to bestow covenant wealth upon.
      b. The eyes of David ran to and fro throughout the whole earth searching for an heir of his covenant brother to lavish covenant wealth upon.
      c. How much more is God searching for us!

B. **Deuteronomy 8:18—God Gives Us the Power to Get Wealth in Order to Establish His Covenant With Us and His Covenant on Earth**
   1. NLT: "Remember the Lord your God. He is the one who gives you power to be successful, in order to fulfill the covenant He confirmed to your ancestors with an oath."
   2. Prosperity is a sign of our covenant with God.
   3. Zechariah 8:13 (NLT): "…I will rescue you and will make you both a symbol and a source of blessing."
   4. Genesis 17:1-8: God covenanted with Abraham to make him rich
   5. Galatians 3:13-14, 29—We are heirs of the covenant
      a. Verse 29: "And if ye be Christ's, then are ye Abraham's seed, and heirs according to the promise."

**C. "Covenant of Wealth" Scriptures**
1. Deuteronomy 28:2: "And all these [covenant] blessings shall come on thee, and over-take thee…."
   a. Brenton: "All these blessings shall come upon you and shall find you…."
   b. HEB: "All these blessings shall reach you…."
2. Deuteronomy 28:11: "And the Lord shall make thee plenteous in goods…."
   a. MSG: "God will lavish you with good things…."
   b. AMP: "He will make you to have a surplus of prosperity…."
3. Ecclesiastes 5:19 (NLT): "And it is a good thing to receive wealth from God and the good health to enjoy it."
4. Genesis 15:1: "Fear not Abram: I am your shield and your exceeding great reward."
   a. AMP: "I am your Shield, your abundant compensation, and your reward shall be exceedingly great."
   b. HEB: "I am your rapidly increasing money supply."
5. Hebrews 10:35: "Cast not away therefore your confidence, which hath great recompense of reward."
   a. Recompense of reward (GK) MISTHA-PODOSIA
      i. MISTHA = pay, salary, money, repay a debt, payment of wages due
      ii. PODOS = feet
   b. Money is coming on feet in your direction
   c. "Money cometh to me now!"
6. Psalm 68:19: "Blessed be the Lord, who daily loadeth us with benefits.
   a. Darby: "Blessed be the Lord: day by day He loads us with good."
   b. DRB: "Blessed be the Lord day by day: the God of our salvation will make our journey prosperous to us."
7. Psalm 103:2 (AMP): "Bless the Lord, O my soul, and forget not one of all His (covenant) benefits."

**D. What the Word Tells Us About Famine**
1. Job 5:20, 22 (NLT): "He will save you from death in time of famine…. You will laugh at destruction and famine."
2. Psalm 33:18-19: "Behold, the eye of the Lord is upon them that fear him, upon them that hope in His mercy [NLT—rely on His unfailing love]; to deliver their soul from death, and to keep them alive in famine."
3. Psalm 37:18-19: Even in famine they will have more than enough
   a. HEB: He will supply until no more is needed
4. In famine, we don't just survive—WE THRIVE!
   a. Prosper, flourish, succeed, advance
   b. Grow vigorously
   c. Increase in goods and estate

# DAYS OF PROSPERITY
**Pastor George Pearsons**

## The Floodgates of Heaven

### Day #17

A. **Malachi 3:10-12—Bring Ye All the Tithes**
1. Verse 10: "…Open you the windows of heaven, and pour you out a blessing, that there shall not be room enough to receive it."
2. *Brenton:* "…See if I will not open to you the torrents of heaven, and pour out my blessing upon you, until ye are satisfied."
3. CEV: "…I will open the windows of heaven and flood you with blessing after blessing."
4. DRB: "…If I open not unto you the flood-gates of heaven, and pour you out a blessing even to abundance."
5. NIV: "…See if I will not throw open the floodgates of heaven and pour out so much blessing that there will not be room enough to store it."

B. **Genesis 7:11-12, 17-20—The Floodgates of Heaven**
1. Verse 11: The windows of heaven were opened (HEB)—floodgates
2. *Blessing* (HEB) = abundant, liberal, excessive prosperity
3. Verse 17-20: Replace the word *waters* with *The Blessing*
   a. Verse 17: "And the flood was forty days upon the earth; and [The Blessing (the abundant, liberal, excessive prosperity)] increased, and bare up the ark, and it was lift up above the earth."
   b. Verse 18: "And [The Blessing] prevailed, and was increased greatly upon the earth; and the ark went upon the face of [The Blessing]."
   c. Verse 19: "And [The Blessing] prevailed exceedingly upon the earth; and all the high hills, that were under the whole heaven, were covered [with The Blessing]."
   d. Verse 20: "[Twenty-two and a half feet] upward did [The Blessing] prevail; and the mountains were covered [with The Blessing]."
4. The Blessing covers 22 1/2 feet from the highest peak with abundant, liberal, excessive prosperity
5. Believe for a constant, steady, nonstop outpouring of God's abundant, liberal, excessive prosperity

**C. Ezekiel 34:25-27—Showers of Blessing**

1. "I will make with them a covenant of peace, and will cause the evil beasts to cease out of the land: and they shall dwell safely in the wilderness, and sleep in the woods. And I will make them and the places around my hill a blessing; and I will cause the shower to come down in his season; there shall be showers of blessing. And the tree of the field shall yield her fruit, and the earth shall yield her increase, and they shall be safe in their land, and shall know that I am the Lord."
2. Not the "light shower" that religion has taught
3. *Shower* (HEB) = to shower, rain and pour down violently
4. *Shower*
   a. A falling of things from the air in thick succession
   b. A copious supply—abundant, plentiful, full, rich
   c. A falling of things in great and large quantities
5. When we tithe, we should be expecting a nonstop downpour and torrent of abundant, liberal, excessive prosperity and provision coming down violently in thick succession from the floodgates of heaven!

**D. The Effects of Tithing**

1. The tithe protects our money
2. Tithing places us under warranty
3. Tithing extends our warranty

**E. The Effects of a Flood**

1. A dam contains the water
2. When the dam breaks, the water is no longer contained—uncontainable
3. It saturates everything
4. "Not a trickle, not a stream, not a river but a flood." —Oral Roberts
5. The tithe places us in "flood stage"

## EAGLE MOUNTAIN
### INTERNATIONAL CHURCH

# DAYS OF PROSPERITY
**Pastor George Pearsons**

## God's Favor and Wealth

### Day #18

**A. What Is the Favor of God?**
1. *Favor* is the same word for *grace*—God's kindness and help extended toward us
2. Promotion, restoration, honor, victory, recognition, preferential treatment and supernatural increase in assets and real estate
3. The favor of God is God personally acting on your behalf doing for you whatever it takes for you to prosper, thrive, flourish and be the success you were created to be
4. The favor of God will cause people to go out of their way to bless you, provide for you, help you, assist you and make special concessions just for you
5. The favor of God will make a way where there is no way, open doors where there are no doors, provide where there is no provision and do the impossible in the midst of the most impossible situations

**B. The Favor of God Will Increase Assets and Real Estate**
1. Psalm 84:11 (AMP): "The Lord God is a Sun and Shield; the Lord bestows [present] grace and favor and [future] glory! No good thing will He withhold from those who walk uprightly."
2. Psalm 44:3: "They got not the land in possession by their own sword, neither did their own arm save them: but thy right hand, and thine arm, and the light of thy countenance, because thou hadst a favour unto them."
3. Deuteronomy 33:23: "And of Naphtali he said, O Naphtali, satisfied with favour, and full with the blessing of the Lord: possess thou the west and the south."
   a. NLT: "…You are rich in favor and full of the Lord's blessings: may you possess the west and the south."
4. Exodus 3:21: "I will give this people favour in the sight of the Egyptians: and it shall come to pass, that, when ye go, ye shall not go empty."
   a. NLT: "…I will see to it that the Egyptians treat you well. They will load you down with gifts so you will not leave empty-handed."
5. Genesis 39:1-6: "And Joseph was brought down to Egypt; and Potiphar, an officer of Pharaoh, captain of the guard, an Egyptian, bought him of the hands of the Ishmaelites, which had brought him down thither. And the Lord was with Joseph, and he was a prosperous man; and he was in the house of his master the Egyptian. And his master saw that the Lord was with him, and that the Lord made all that he

did to prosper in his hand. And Joseph found grace in his sight, and he served him: and he made him overseer over his house, and all that he had he put into his hand. And it came to pass from the time that he had made him overseer in his house, and over all that he had, that the Lord blessed the Egyptian's house for Joseph's sake; and the blessing of the Lord was upon all that he had in the house, and in the field. And he left all that he had in Joseph's hand; and he knew not aught he had, save the bread which he did eat. And Joseph was a goodly person, and well favoured."

**C. Today Is the Day of God's Favor**
1. Luke 4:18-21 (AMP): "The Spirit of the Lord [is] upon Me, because He has anointed Me [the Anointed One, the Messiah] to preach the good news (the Gospel) to the poor; He has sent Me to announce release to the captives and recovery of sight to the blind, to send forth as delivered those who are oppressed [who are downtrodden, bruised, crushed, and broken down by calamity], to proclaim the accepted and acceptable year of the Lord [the day when salvation and the free favors of God profusely abound]. Then He rolled up the book and gave it back to the attendant and sat down; and the eyes of all in the synagogue were gazing [attentively] at Him. And He began to speak to them: Today this Scripture has been fulfilled while you are present and hearing."
2. Psalm 5:12: The favor of God surrounds us
3. Proverbs 14:9: The favor of God is among us
4. Luke 2:14 (NIV): The favor of God rests upon us
5. Genesis 12:2 (AMP): God blesses us with an abundant increase of His favors

**D. Say, "The favor of God is working on my behalf!"**

# DAYS OF PROSPERITY
### Pastor George Pearsons

## The Blessing of the Lord Makes Rich

### Day #19

**A. Proverbs 10:22—The Blessing of the Lord, It Makes Rich, and He Adds No Sorrow With It**
1. AMP: "The Blessing of the Lord—it makes [truly] rich, and He adds no sorrow with it [neither does toiling increase it]."
2. NIV: "The Blessing of the Lord brings wealth, without painful toil for it."
3. *Brenton:* "The Blessing of the Lord is upon the head of the righteous; it enriches him, and grief of heart shall not be added to it."
4. GNB: "It is the Lord's Blessing that makes you wealthy...."
5. Psalm 112: The Bible definition of *rich*

**B. *Rich* Is Not a Dirty Word—It Is a Bible Word**
1. *Rich* (HEB) AWSHAR = accumulate and grow; wax great
2. "If you will learn to follow the inward witness, I will make you rich. I will guide you in all the affairs of life, financial as well as spiritual. I am not opposed to my children being rich; I am opposed to them being covetous. To be rich is to have a full supply and abundant provision." —word from the Lord to Kenneth E. Hagin
3. "You don't live in the spirit just to keep your bills paid and your body well just so you can lay around and watch TV in comfort. God is not prospering us to get us out of debt so we can get into bigger debt. He is not prospering us so we can buy and buy and buy. He is prospering us so we can give and give and give." —Kenneth Copeland
4. "My priorities for prosperity are God first, others second, and me last. We prosper for covenant reasons—not for covetous reasons." —Dr. Leroy Thompson
5. "I am convinced in my mind by my heart that the reason I want money is to do the work of the gospel! Thank You, Lord, for the peace of that revelation. Satan, you will never be able to make me believe, ever again, that the reason I want money is for selfish gain. My God is my provider." —Jeremy Pearsons, 5/6/98 (age 20)
6. My motivation for accumulation is distribution.

**C. 1 Timothy 6:17-18—Charge Them That Are Rich**
1. Don't be high-minded
2. Don't trust in riches, but in the living God
3. Do good

4. Be rich in good works
5. Be ready to distribute, willing to give

**D. Even the World Knows Better**
1. "I have never believed that prosperity is bad or something to be shunned."
   —Donald Trump
2. Secular books written on the subject of prosperity
   a. *The Road to Wealth*
   b. *9 Steps to Financial Freedom*
   c. *The Guide to Becoming Rich*
   d. *The Science of Getting Rich*
   e. *Millionaire Maker*
   f. *Start Late, Finish Rich*
   g. *Retire Young, Retire Rich*
   h. *Zero Debt*
   i. *Rich and Happy*
   j. *Why We Want You to Be Rich*
   k. *Dare to Be Rich*
   l. *Think and Grow Rich*
   m. *Smart Women Finish Rich*
   n. *Rich Women*
3. How much more should we be walking in The Blessing of God's covenant wealth?
4. 2 Corinthians 8:9 (NLT): "You know the generous grace of our Lord Jesus Christ. Though he was rich, yet for your sakes he became poor, so that by his poverty he could make you rich."
5. He wants us to get way beyond a "paycheck-to-paycheck, barely surviving" lifestyle

**E. Ezekiel 16:7—Our God is THE "Millionaire Maker"**
1. "I have caused thee to multiply as the bud of the field, and thou hast increased and waxen great, and thou art come to excellent ornaments…."
2. *Excellent ornaments* (HEB) = fine outfits
3. I have caused you to multiply (HEB) = I have made you a million
4. Proverbs 8:17-21 (AMP): Riches and honor are with the Lord, enduring wealth, (KJV—durable riches) and righteousness. The Lord causes those who love Him to inherit true riches and He fills my treasuries
5. Deuteronomy 8:18 (NLT): "Remember the Lord your God. He is the one who gives you power to be successful, in order to fulfill the covenant he confirmed with your ancestors with an oath."

**F. Genesis 14:22-23:** "And Abram said to the king of Sodom, I have lift up mine hand unto the Lord, the most high God, the possessor of heaven and earth, that I will not take from a thread even to a shoelatchet, and that I will not take any thing that is thine, lest thou shouldest say, I have made Abram rich."

# DAYS OF PROSPERITY
**Pastor George Pearsons**

## The Heart of Prosperity

### Day #20

**A.** *True Prosperity* **Defined by Kenneth Copeland**
1. True prosperity is the ability to use the power of God to meet the needs of mankind in every realm of life—spirit, soul, body, financially, socially
2. True prosperity is when you make it your need to get salvation into the hands of people and when you make it your purpose to feed the gospel to the unsaved
3. True prosperity is the ability to look a man in the eye in his moment of impossibility and take his needs on as your own
4. True prosperity is walking with God to be able and equipped to do for others whatever He needs done, whenever He needs it done and with whatever He needs it done
5. True prosperity is not for keeping your bills paid and your body well just so you can lie around and watch TV in comfort. God is not prospering us to get us out of debt so we can get into bigger debt. He is not prospering us so we can buy and buy and buy. He is prospering us so we can give and give and give.

**B. Our Motivation for Accumulation Is Distribution**
1. Genesis 12:2 (AMP): "I will make of you a great nation, and I will bless you [with abundant increase of favors] and make your name famous and distinguished, and you will be a blessing [dispensing good to others]."
2. Philippians 2:4: "Look not every man on his own things, but every man also on the things of others."
   a. AMP: "…Be concerned for not [merely] [your] own interests, but also each for the interests of others."
3. Galatians 6:10 (KNOX): "Let us practice generosity to all while the opportunity is ours, and above all, to those who are one family with us in the household of faith."
   a. Creflo Dollar emptied his entire account and sowed the money toward KCM's airplane
   b. He put KCM's need above his own
   c. Kenneth and Gloria Copeland have sown over 30 airplanes, placing others' needs above their own

4. 1 Corinthians 10:24: "Let no man seek his own, but every man another's wealth."
   a. JBP/WOR: Let no man set his own advantage as his objective, but let each seek the good of others.
5. "A man's life consists not in the abundance of the things he possesses, but in the abundance of the things he sows." —Kenneth Copeland

## C. Giving Is at the Very Heart of Prosperity
1. 2 Corinthians 9:11 (NIV): "[As a result of your giving] you will be enriched in every way so that you can be generous on every occasion, and through us your generosity will result in thanksgiving to God."
2. AMP: "Thus you will be enriched in all things and in every way, so that you can be generous, and [your generosity as it is] administered by us will bring forth thanksgiving to God."
3. Billye Brim shared that during the "Restore Honor" meeting in Washington, D.C., a rabbi shared that God's Word commands us to make money because we are God's stewards on earth with the responsibility to distribute His wealth.

# DAYS OF PROSPERITY
**Pastor George Pearsons**

## All of Heaven's Reserves

### Day #21

A. **2 Chronicles 20:20:** "…Believe in the Lord your God, so shall ye be established; believe his prophets, so shall ye prosper."
   1. Prophetic words are given for our benefit
   2. They give us direction, instruction, correction
   3. Amos 3:7: "Surely the Lord God will do nothing, but he revealeth his secret unto his servants the prophets."
   4. They give us light for the path ahead
   5. Word from the Lord through Kenneth Copeland concerning 2011
      a. Prayer Mountain Prayer Conference
      b. October 28, 2010

B. **"2011—Straight From Heaven" Prophetic Word**
*Word from the Lord through Brother Copeland, October 28, 2010*

Have no fear of this world. I have overcome it, saith the Lord. I left nothing—absolutely nothing—that faith won't overcome. I left it no power. I left it no strength. It has NO-THING over you.

So, hear this about 2011. What will it be like? I will tell you exactly what it will be like, saith the Lord.

Whatever you compromise to keep, you will lose. So be bold in My Word. Be strong and stand up for something. Stand up for the word of faith. Stand up for the fact that God loves you and will take care of you and will continue to take care of you.

And I can tell you this. I have said it before and I will say it again, and again, and again, and again—times and times again. I will say it.

*For 2011—everything is going to be ALL right!*

A new day is coming and it is here now. Everything is going to be ALL right. I said everything is going to be all right.

For all of you who will take My Word and stand on it, saith the Lord—the kingdom is for you, the angels are for you, all of heaven's reserves are at your call. Rise up and be counted among those who carry faith, live by faith, walk in love and declare that God so loved the world that He gave. Relax and rest and rejoice, because everything is going to be ALL right. Everything is going to be ALL right. Everything is going to be ALL right.

### 2011—Straight From Heaven

A wealthy place. A good place. THE BLESSING is the place to be. 2011—you will see it come to pass.

It will be said of that year among those who count themselves in the household of God and in the word of faith, and those who have stood up and believed My Word and have walked in it all these years—it is going to be the easiest year you have ever had in your life.

Things are going to flow and things are going to just move and flow along. It will seem like you have been caught up in a wave of glory. It will just go and it will go and it will go, and you will begin to learn how to just say things and they come to pass. You will walk in the goodness and in the grace and in the mercy of God.

All that you should be, will be.

All that you could be, will be.

And all that shouldn't be, won't be, because God is alive and well—and so are you!

C. **"All of Heaven's Reserves Are at Your Call"**
   1. James 1:17: "Every good gift and every perfect gift is from above, and cometh down from the Father of lights, with whom is no variableness, neither shadow of turning."
      a. AMP: "Every good gift and perfect (free, large, full) gift is from above…."
      b. GNB: "Every good gift and every perfect present comes from heaven…."
      c. MSG: "Every desirable and beneficial gift comes out of heaven…."
   2. Psalm 78:23-29 (NLT): "But he commanded the skies to open; he opened the doors of heaven. He rained down manna for them to eat; he gave them bread from heaven. They ate the food of angels! God gave them all they could hold. He released the east wind in the heavens and guided the south wind by his mighty power. He rained down meat as thick as dust—birds as plentiful as the sand on the seashore! He caused the birds to fall within their camp and all around their tents. The people ate their fill. He gave them what they craved."
   3. Philippians 4:19: "But my God shall supply all your need according to His riches in glory by Christ Jesus."
      a. BBE: "And my God will give you all you have need of from the wealth of His glory in Christ Jesus."

      b. GK: My God will liberally supply, fill to the full, cram, furnish, satisfy, finish and complete all of your needs, employment, requirements, lack and business according to His riches, His wealth, His money and His possessions in glory by Christ Jesus.

4. Deuteronomy 28:12: "The Lord shall open unto thee his good treasure, the heaven to give the rain unto thy land in his season, and to bless all the work of thine hand…."
      a. *Treasure* (HEB) = depository, armory, treasure house
      b. AMP: His good treasury
      c. ASV: Treasure of the heavens
      d. BBE: His storehouses in heaven
      e. CEV: The storehouses of the skies
      f. MSG: "God will throw open the doors of His sky vaults and pour rain on your land on schedule…."

5. Malachi 3:10: "Bring ye all the tithes into the storehouse, that there may be meat in mine house, and prove me now herewith, saith the Lord of hosts, if I will not open you the windows of heaven, and pour you out a blessing, that there shall not be room enough to receive it."
      a. *Brenton:* The torrents of heaven
      b. NIV: "…See if I will not throw open the floodgates of heaven and pour you out a blessing, even to abundance."

6. Ezekiel 34:25-27: "…I will cause the shower to come down in his season; there shall be showers of blessing."
      a. *Shower* (HEB) = pour down violently
      b. A falling of things from the air in thick succession and in great and large quantities.
      c. When we tithe, we should expect a nonstop downpour and a torrent of abundant, liberal, excessive prosperity and provision coming down violently in thick succession through the floodgates of heaven!
      d. "Not a trickle, not a stream, not a river but a flood." —Oral Roberts

**D. "All of Heaven's Reserves Are at Your Call"—So Call in the Reserves!**

**EAGLE MOUNTAIN**

INTERNATIONAL CHURCH

## DAYS OF PROSPERITY
**Pastor George Pearsons**

## Freedom From Financial Fear

### Day #22

**A. Everything Is Going to Be All Right!**
1. Images of fear are all around us
2. Fear of financial failure is trying to grip people's hearts
3. We must aggressively take our stand against financial fear and believe that everything is going to be all right
4. "Everything is going to be all right in the household of faith. Don't feed fear and trouble into your life and into your mouth. No! Quit living in that house. Get back over here in the household of faith. Feed on My Word and not on the bread of sorrow. Feed on My Word. Everything's going to be all right." —word of the Lord through Kenneth Copeland, Southwest Believers' Convention, August 6, 2010
5. "Have no fear of this world. I have overcome it," saith the Lord. "I left nothing— absolutely nothing—that faith won't overcome. I left it no power. I left it no strength. It has NO-THING over you." —word of the Lord through Kenneth Copeland, Prayer Mountain Meeting, October 28, 2010

**B. Psalm 34:1-4:** "…I Sought the Lord, and he heard me, and delivered me from all my fears."
1. Faith and fear are expectations
   a. Faith expects the best
   b. Fear expects the worst
2. Faith and fear are magnets
   a. Faith is a magnet that draws provision
   b. Fear is a magnet that draws lack
      i. Proverbs 29:25: "The fear of man bringeth a snare…."
      ii. Job 3:25: "The thing which I greatly feared is come upon me…."
      iii. HEB: I feared a fear and it came on me
3. The contrast between faith and fear
   a. Romans 10:17: Faith for finances comes by hearing the Word of God about prosperity and fear of lack comes by hearing the lies of the devil about poverty.

  b. Hebrews 11:1: Faith is the substance of prosperity hoped for, the evidence of prosperity not seen. Fear is the substance of poverty dreaded, the evidence of poverty not seen.

  c. 1 John 5:4: This is the victory that overcomes lack—even our faith. This is the defeat that overcomes us—even our fear.

 4. We must adopt a "zero-tolerance policy" toward any form of fear.

  a. "No fear here"

  b. Develop a bulldog faith

 5. Kellie declared, "I refuse to fear," when her daughter Lyndsey was given a terrible report about spinal meningitis

  a. The whole situation changed from that moment on

  b. Fear left and faith came on the scene

  c. You must use your faith in the same way over your finances

## C. I Refuse to Fear Over Finances!

 1. 2 Timothy 1:7: I have not been given the spirit of fear over my finances—but of power and love and of a sound mind

 2. Isaiah 41:10: God said, "Fear not," for He is with me. I am not dismayed over my financial condition; He is my God—my Provider and my Supplier. Everything is going to be all right!

 3. Psalm 27:3: Though a host of bills should encamp against me, my heart shall not fear

 4. Psalm 112:7: I shall not be afraid of economic conditions; my heart is fixed, trusting in the Lord. My heart is established. I shall not be afraid.

 5. James 4:7: I resist the fear of lack and the fear of lack must flee!

## D. My Confession of Faith

I refuse to fear.

I am not moved by what I see.

I am not fearful over my financial future.

God is my source of provision.

He provides cars to drive, food to eat, clothes to wear, places to live and everything else I need in liberal supply.

I am not subject to the times.

I live in the household of faith, not the dungeon of fear.

My household is thriving, and not just surviving.

My household is flourishing and not failing.

Every bill is paid, every need is met and every debt is wiped out.

I walk by faith and not by fear, in Jesus' Name!

**EAGLE MOUNTAIN**

INTERNATIONAL CHURCH

# DAYS OF PROSPERITY
**Pastor George Pearsons**

## My Faith for Provision Works All the Time

### Day #23

**A. Galatians 6:9:** "Let us not be weary in well doing: for in due season we shall reap, if we faint not."

    1. AMP: "Let us not lose heart and grow weary and faint in acting nobly and doing right, for in due time and at the appointed season we shall reap, if we do not loosen and relax our courage and faint."

    2. A note to Pastor George:
"Thank you, Pastor George, for teaching us about reaping. We have been going back over your first '10 Days of Prosperity' on the Internet. It is really blessing us. We had been asking the same question over and over again—'We tithe and give, but we are not seeing results. Why isn't it working for us?' After reviewing your series, we are very encouraged! Our faith is back on track and is now working again!"

    3. Many ask the same question: "Why isn't it working for me?"

    4. When they tithe and sow and don't see results, they get discouraged, and wonder why it doesn't work

    5. They don't realize that their harvest is right around the faith corner

**B. Hebrews 10:23, 35-36: We Must Stand Firm in Faith Until We See the Results**

    1. Verse 23: "Let us hold fast the profession of our faith without wavering; (for he is faithful that promised)."

        a. AMP: "So let us seize and hold fast and retain without wavering the hope we cherish and confess and our acknowledgement of it, for He Who promised is reliable (sure) and faithful to His word."

        b. NLT: "Let us hold tightly without wavering to the hope we affirm, for God can be trusted to keep his promise."

    2. We must stay encouraged and continue to use our faith

    3. Verses 35-36: "Cast not away therefore your confidence, which has great recompense of reward. For ye have need of patience, that, after ye have done the will of God, ye might receive the promise."

        a. AMP: "Do not, therefore, fling away your fearless confidence, for it carries a great and glorious compensation of reward. For you have need of steadfast patience and endurance, so that you may perform and fully accomplish the will of God, and thus receive and carry away [and enjoy to the full] what is promised."

      b. Cast not away your boldness of speech and confession.

   4. Hebrews 6:12: Be imitators of those who through faith and patience inherit the promises.

   5. *Patience*

      a. Not knuckling under and hunkering down until the storm passes over

      b. Maintaining your stand in spite of the circumstances

      c. Being constant all the time

      d. The ability to see the results before you have them

**C. Proverbs 18:21: Life and Death Are in the Power of the Tongue**

   1. Encourage your faith by speaking life over your tithing and giving.

   2. *Tithe*—Declare that the windows of heaven are opened over your life.

   3. *Seed*—Declare that your giving is producing an extreme, maximum, overflowing harvest.

   4. "My faith is alive, activated and energized."

   5. "My faith for provision is working for me all the time!"

      a. Luke 6:38: "I give and it is given to me!"

      b. Galatians 6:7: "I reap what I sow!"

      c. Psalm 112:2: "My seed is mighty upon the earth!"

**EAGLE MOUNTAIN**
INTERNATIONAL CHURCH

## DAYS OF PROSPERITY
**Pastor George Pearsons**

## I Heartily Agree With God

### Day #24

**A.  Romans 4:18-21: Abraham Heartily Agreed With God**
1.  Verse 18: "Who against hope believed in hope, that he might become the father of many nations, according to that which was spoken, So shall thy seed be."
2.  *According to* (GK) = Hearty agreement
    a.  Total, complete, unquestioning, unreserved agreement
    b.  Verse 20: "He staggered not at the promise of God through unbelief…."
    c.  Verse 21: He was so fully persuaded that what God had promised in His Word, He was totally able to perform
3.  Abraham was in hearty agreement with what God had spoken to him about being the father of many nations
4.  Verse 18 (MSG): "When everything was hopeless, Abraham believed anyway, deciding to live not on the basis of what he saw he couldn't do but on what God said he would do…."
5.  "I am in hearty agreement with what God has already said in His Word about my prosperity."

**B.  I Heartily Agree With God**
1.  Deuteronomy 8:18: It is the Lord my God who gives me the power to get wealth in order to establish His covenant in the earth
2.  Deuteronomy 28: I heartily agree with The Blessing of Abraham
    a.  Verse 2: All these blessings come on me and overtake me
    b.  Verse 8: The commanded blessing is upon my storehouses
    c.  Verse 11 (AMP): The Lord makes me to have a surplus of prosperity
    d.  Verse 12 (AMP): The Lord has opened to me His rich treasury
3.  Psalm 35:27: The Lord takes pleasure in my prosperity
4.  Psalm 36:8: I am abundantly satisfied with the prosperity of God's house and I drink out of the river of His pleasures
    a.  AMP: I relish and feast on the abundance of God's house
5.  Psalm 65:11 (NLT): You crown my year with a bountiful harvest and even the hard pathways overflow with abundance

6. Psalm 66:12: God has brought me out into a wealthy place—a broad and open place of His abundance and refreshment
7. Psalm 68:19: God daily loads me with benefits
8. Psalm 85:12: The Lord shall give me that which is good and our land shall yield her increase
    a. NLT: The Lord pours down His blessings. Our land will yield its bountiful harvest
9. Psalm 92:12: The righteous shall flourish like the palm tree
    a. *Flourish* (HEB) = Increase; enlarge; become extremely successful; enter into a state of prosperity; grow exuberantly; increase in wealth, favor and honor
    b. I am increasing, enlarging, becoming extremely successful and have entered into a state of prosperity
    c. I am growing exuberantly and increasing in wealth, favor and honor
10. Psalm 112:3: Wealth and riches are in my house
    a. JERU: There are riches and wealth for my family
    b. AMP: Prosperity and welfare are in my house
11. Psalm 115:14: The Lord is increasing me more and more—me and my children
12. Proverbs 8:21 (AMP): Because I love the Lord, He causes me to inherit true riches and He fills my treasures
13. Proverbs 13:22: I leave an inheritance to my children's children and the wealth of the sinner is laid up for me
14. Proverbs 19:14: House and riches are my inheritance
15. Proverbs 24:3-4 (AMP): Through skillful and godly wisdom, my house, my life, my family and my home are built. By understanding they are established on a sound and good foundation. And by knowledge are the chambers of every area filled with all precious and pleasant riches.
16. Ecclesiastes 5:19 (NLT): I receive wealth from God and the health to enjoy it. It is a good thing!
17. Isaiah 48:17: It is the Lord my God who teaches me to profit and leads me in the way that I should go
18. Malachi 3:10: The windows of heaven are open over me and God is pouring out a blessing that I cannot contain
19. 2 Corinthians 8:9 (NLT): Jesus became poor in order that by His poverty I am enriched and abundantly supplied
    a. By Jesus' stripes, I am healed
    b. By Jesus' poverty, I am rich
20. 2 Peter 1:3 (AMP): His divine power has bestowed upon me all the things that are requisite and suited to life and godliness

**C. "I heartily agree with everything that God has said in His Word about my prosperity!"**

# EAGLE MOUNTAIN

INTERNATIONAL CHURCH

## DAYS OF PROSPERITY
### Pastor George Pearsons

## The Power of Your Words

**A. Five Vital Truths About Words**
1. There is nothing in this earth so great or so powerful, including the physical body, that cannot be turned around by our words. You can turn around any situation with your words.
2. The entire course of nature (future and destiny) and the circumstances surrounding every human being are controlled by that person's words.
3. We don't have a choice whether or not we live by words. We do, however, have a choice of what words we live by.
4. If your mouth will feed your heart the word of faith when you don't need it—your heart will feed your mouth the word of faith when you do need it.
5. We appropriate what is ours in Christ by making God's Word a daily part of our vocabulary. We are to confess what we can do in Christ, who we are in Christ, and what we have in Christ.

**B. Proverbs 22:17-18 (AMP):** "Listen (consent and submit) to the words of the wise, and apply your mind to my knowledge; for it will be pleasant if you keep them in your mind [believing them]; your lips will be accustomed to [confessing] them."

**C. Isaiah 58:13: Don't speak your own words**

**D. Psalm 17:4 (AMP):** "Concerning the works of men, by the word of Your lips I have avoided the ways of the violent (the paths of the destroyer)."

# DAYS OF PROSPERITY
**Pastor George Pearsons**

## Words Defined

*A man's belly shall be satisfied with the fruit of his mouth;*
*and with the increase of his lips shall he be filled.*
*Death and life are in the power of the tongue:*
*and they that love it shall eat the fruit thereof.*
Proverbs 18:20-21

1. Words are God's method of operation by which He accomplishes His will, purpose and desire
2. Words set spiritual laws in motion
    a. The law of sin and death
    b. The law of the Spirit of life in Christ Jesus
3. Words are the most important things in the universe
    a. Faith-filled words will put you over
    b. Fear-filled words will defeat you
4. Words are spiritual containers that carry power
    a. Carry love and faith
    b. Carry hate and fear
5. Words are seeds sown with your mouth that produce after their own kind
6. Words are the process starters of life
7. Words are the building blocks with which you construct your life and future
8. Words set the cornerstones of your life
9. Words set boundaries, which confine or release you
10. Words have creative ability
    a. They create the realities you see
    b. God's Word—the incorruptible seed, has within it the ability and DNA to cause itself to come to pass
11. Words program the human spirit for success or failure
12. Words of God, conceived in the heart, spoken out the mouth, become a spiritual force that release faith—which is the creative ability of God
13. Words establish strongholds, break habits, change things, redirect thought patterns
14. Words point you in whatever direction they are aimed and released
15. Words set the course of your life

16. Words determine your future, your health, your wealth and your place in eternity—you are the prophet of your own life
17. Words arrive at your future before you do
18. Words create desires and transmit images that you will eventually live out
19. Words frame your world
20. Words spoken today become a living reality tomorrow
21. Words give permission and license to spiritual forces to work for you or against you
22. Words can turn around any situation
23. Words make demands on the blessing or the curse—whichever you call for
24. Words are goal setters that give direction and establish destination
25. Words are our method of operation, by which God accomplishes His will, purpose and desire for our lives

*Set a watch (guard), O Lord, before my mouth; keep the door of my lips.*
Psalm 141:3

# EAGLE MOUNTAIN
### INTERNATIONAL CHURCH

## DAYS OF PROSPERITY
### Pastor George Pearsons

## Money Cometh to Me, Now!

### Day #25

**A. A Prophetic Word for the Body of Christ from Dr. Leroy Thompson**
1. Dr. Thompson was shopping at the grocery store.
2. While in the checkout line, the person ahead of Dr. Thompson turned to him and said, "Money goes." Dr. Thompson answered, "Money goes."
3. On the way to the car, the Lord corrected him and said, "Money comes."
4. The Lord told him that this was a prophetic word for the Body of Christ
5. The Lord said we are to declare, "Money cometh to me, now!"

**B. Romans 4:17: We call in things that be not as though they were.**
1. RSV: Call into existence the things that do not exist
2. *Call* (GK) KALEO = To summon
3. *Summons*—An authoritative command demanding someone to appear
4. Jury duty summons—"You are hereby notified to appear."
5. When you say "Money cometh to me, now," you are actually saying, "Money—you are hereby notified to appear."

**C. Rick Renner's Scriptural Basis for "Money Cometh to Me, Now!"**
1. Rick Renner showed me scriptural proof for "money cometh."
   (See Rick's handwritten notes attached)
2. Hebrews 10:35: "Cast not away therefore your confidence, which has great recompense of reward."
3. *Recompense of reward* (GK) = MISTHAPODOSIA
   a. MISTHA = Pay, salary, money, recompense, restitution
   b. PODOSIA = Feet or foot (podiatrist)
4. Translations
   a. "Money is coming on feet in your direction."
   b. "Money is traveling your way."
   c. "Money is coming."

5.  Provision is running to me
    a.  Luke 6:38: "Give, and it shall be given unto you; good measure, pressed down, and shaken together, and running over, shall men give unto your bosom…."
    b.  Deuteronomy 28:2: "And all these blessing shall come thee, and overtake thee…."
    c.  Psalm 23:6: "Surely goodness and mercy shall follow me all the days of my life…."
        i.  *Follow* (HEB) = Pursue, chase, run after

## D. Confession

Money, I summon you.
I hereby call you to appear.
You have feet and you are coming my way.
I am a money magnet.
Money cometh to me, NOW, in Jesus' Name.

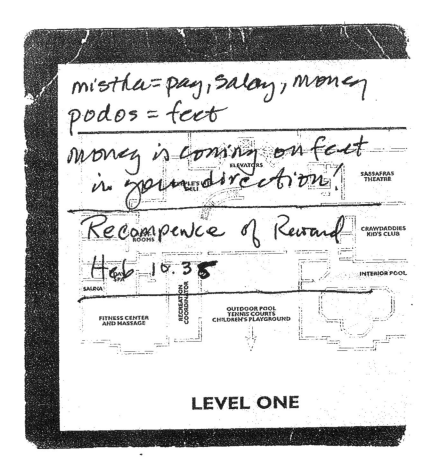

mistha = pay, salary, money
podos = feet

money is coming on feet
in your direction!

Recompence of Reward

Heb 10.35

LEVEL ONE

*Second Draft*

μισθαποδοσια

= misthapodosia

misth a — podos

(pay, salary, money) — (feet or foot – "podiatrist")

"money is coming on feet in your direction."

"money is traveling your way.

✳ "money is coming." ✳

recompense
reparation
restitution
reward

**EAGLE MOUNTAIN**

INTERNATIONAL CHURCH

# DAYS OF PROSPERITY
### Pastor George Pearsons

## Our Source of Supply

### Day #26

A. **"What About 2011?"**
*Word from the Lord through Brother Copeland, November 11, 2010*

Now, what about 2011? What is in store? What is God saying about it?

It will be a time of changes. It will be the best of times and it will be the worst of times. The biggest amount of change will come in the harvest. What is harvest to one man is judgment to another one because both of them are the manifestations of seed. Seed grows up and becomes. And when the wages of sin, or the harvest of sin, is death, you just stay with it and it will kill you.

The sower sows the Word. Well, the harvest of that is abundance and plenty—the hundredfold return.

And here is what I heard the Lord say:

For those who insist on compromising the Word and insist on it. I am not talking about the world. I mean, that is what they do all the time. Sinners sin. You understand? That is what they do best. But, I am talking about people who have an allegiance to the Lord Jesus Christ, born-again children of God who continue and insist on compromising the Word.

"Ah, yes, Brother Copeland. I know the Bible says that but you just don't understand my situation." "Ah, yes, Brother Copeland. Yes, I know the Bible says that, but you know, I believe it will be all right with the Lord."

Those who insist and persist in disobedience and the compromising of the Word, whatever you compromise to keep, you will lose it. And the difference is, in 2011, in many cases, it will be taken from you right before your eyes. And of course, it is not God who takes it from you. It is the devil. He is the thief. He comes to steal, kill and destroy. God is not taking things away from you. The devil takes them and blames it on God. He will get preachers to preach that to you, but it isn't true.

Now, for those who insist on keeping the love commandment at any price, and those who insist on living by faith and giving God praise and glory, everything is going to be All-Right. That is what I heard the Lord say. Everything is going to be All-Right. Every thing. All-Right. It is going to right-en up.

Straighten up.

Don't look to the government for your supply. Don't look to other people for your supply. No, no. Pastors, don't look to your congregations for your supply.

Jesus is our Source, hallelujah. The blessing of Abraham is our supply. Praise God!

The Word is our supply. Amen.

Now, to walk in that, oh my goodness. You are going to have to pay attention. You are going to have to listen on purpose. Take time to pray and listen to God.

Jesus said, "I only say those things I hear My Father say, and I only do those things I see My Father do." Note, that should be all of us the same way.

Not what we see someone else do or hear someone else say. We take a message someone preaches. We take the written Word of God as the very Word of Jesus, the very Word of the living God. Amen. It is God speaking to me, but there are moments and times when you need to just hush and quit trying to make up and do all your praying on your own, and be quiet and say, "Sir, what should I say at this moment? What should I do? My ears are open and my eyes are open. I am listening."

**B. Our Source of Supply**
1. "Don't look to the government for your supply."
2. "Don't look to other people for your supply."
3. "Pastors, don't look to your congregations for your supply."
4. "Jesus is our Source of supply."
5. "The Blessing of Abraham is our source of supply."
6. "The Word is our source of supply."
7. "My God is the source of all my supply."
   a. This must be ingrained in our thinking
   b. Especially during economic times like these

**C. Settle This Today: God Is My Source!**
1. *Source*—Point of origin
   a. The beginning place
   b. Where something can be traced back to
2. *Supply*—Provision, inventory, stock
3. Our source of supply is the point of origin for the fulfillment of all our needs

4. Philippians 4:19: "My God shall supply all your need according to His riches in glory by Christ Jesus."
    a. BBE: "My God will give you all you have need of from the wealth of his glory in Christ Jesus."
    b. AMP: "My God will liberally supply (fill to the full) your every need according to His riches in glory in Christ Jesus."
5. I settle this today:
    a. Jesus is the Source of my supply
    b. The Blessing of Abraham is the source of my supply
    c. The Word of God is the source of my supply
    d. God is the source of my supply!

# EAGLE MOUNTAIN
### INTERNATIONAL CHURCH

## DAYS OF PROSPERITY
**Pastor George Pearsons**

## The Hundredfold Return

### Day #27

**A. Mark 10:28-30: He Shall Receive an Hundredfold**
(Quotes from Gloria Copeland's book, *God's Will Is Prosperity)*
   1. Verses 28-30: "Peter said to him, See, we have given up everything, and come after you. Jesus said, Truly I say to you, There is no man who has given up house, or brothers, or sisters, or mother, or father, or children, or land, because of me and the good news, who will not get a hundred times as much now in this time, houses, and brothers, and sisters, and mothers, and children, and land—though with great troubles; and, in the world to come, eternal life."
   2. "How great the hundredfold return is: give $1 and receive $100!"
   3. "Where in the natural world are you offered the return of 100 times your investment?"
       a. "If you double your money, you do well."
       b. "If you receive 10 times your investment, it is a marvelous deal."
       c. "But who talks in terms of receiving 100 times your investment?"
   4. "After I let what the Word offers us in the hundredfold return become a reality to me, the Lord led me to continually give thanks for it every time I thought about it."
       a. "I would say, 'Thank You, Father, for the hundredfold return offered in Your Word.'"
       b. "It is such a generous return and it belongs to me."
   5. "I would say any faith words of praise that came into my spirit in regard to continually thanking God for the hundredfold return."
       a. "This thanksgiving kept my faith active and operative to receive."
       b. "Continually confessing the hundredfold return causes the seed of Mark 10:29-30 to grow."

**B. Keep Your Faith Active All the Time**
   1. Mark 10:30: Now in this time
       a. GW: Here in this life
   2. "I realized that the hundredfold return is continually working, coming to me as long as I keep my faith active in its behalf."

3. "None of the blessings of God work automatically, even though they belong to us. They become manifested in our lives as we exercise our faith to receive them."
4. "Healing belongs to every believer, but that great blessing is enjoyed only by those who exercise their faith to receive it."
5. "In the same way, the hundredfold return is a powerful force in the believer's financial blessing, but you have to release your faith to receive all that the Word offers you. The force of faith for the hundredfold return must be applied by the Word of God in your heart and by the confession of your mouth."

**C. The Hundredfold Return Is Working for Me All the Time!**
1. Kenneth and Gloria had been attending a convention in Hawaii
2. On the morning of their departure, Gloria went to the restaurant to get a table
3. A man stepped in front of her and took the table that should have been hers
4. Gloria ended up having to get a table in the very back of the restaurant
5. A woman came up to Gloria and took a ring off her finger, gave it to Gloria and said, "God told me to give this to you. I had been impressed for several days to do this. I asked the Lord during the meeting if that He wanted me to give Gloria Copeland the ring, please have her sit next to me at breakfast in the morning."
6. The ring was stunning and unusual—two squares of emeralds and diamonds set in gold. The two squares rotated as her hand moved. Gloria received it and prayed for the woman.
7. Then she remembered the hundredfold return. The last time they were in Hawaii, at the very same hotel, the Lord impressed Gloria to give someone a diamond ring. When she gave it, she believed for the hundredfold return. The hundredfold was working for her all along.
8. As Gloria looked at the rotating squares of the ring, the Lord impressed her that this ring was to be a reminder that the hundredfold return is continually working for her all the time.
9. Continually keep your faith activated for the hundredfold return
10. Continually confess, "The hundredfold return is working for me all the time!"

**EAGLE MOUNTAIN**

INTERNATIONAL CHURCH

# DAYS OF PROSPERITY
**Pastor George Pearsons**

## Put Your Prosperity Angels to Work

### Day #28

**A. Three-Point Provision Outline by Kenneth E. Hagin**
1. Claim whatever you need
2. Declare: "Satan, take your hands off my money!"
3. Declare: "Ministering spirits, go and cause my money to come!"
4. Our angels are ready to go to work for us
5. "For all of you who will take My Word and stand on it," saith the Lord, "the kingdom is for you, the angels are for you, and all of heaven's reserves are at your call."
   —*word from the Lord through Brother Copeland, October 28, 2010*

**B. Hebrews 1:14:** "Are they not all ministering spirits, sent forth to minister for them who shall be heirs of salvation?"
1. AMP: "Are not the angels all ministering spirits (servants) sent out in the service [of God for the assistance] of those who are to inherit salvation?"
2. Galatians 3:29: "And if ye be Christ's, then are ye Abraham's seed, and heirs according to the promise."
3. We are heirs of salvation—deliverance, preservation, soundness and prosperity
4. The angels of God have been sent to perform whatever is necessary to establish God's covenant in the earth
5. The angels have been sent to serve us
   a. 1 Kings 19:5-6: "As [Elijah] lay and slept under a juniper tree, behold, then an angel touched him, and said unto him, Arise and eat. And he looked, and, behold, there was a cake baken on the coals, and a cruse of water at his head. And he did eat and drink…."
   b. Elijah was gently awakened to the scent of juniper mingled with the aroma of freshly baked pastry—what service!

**C. Psalm 103:20-21—The Angels Are Awaiting Our Command**
1. Verses 20-21: "Bless the Lord, ye His angels, that excel in strength, that do His commandments, hearkening unto the voice of His word. Bless ye the Lord, all ye His hosts; ye ministers of His, that do His pleasure."

2. There is no shortage of angelic help
    a. Hebrews 12:22 An innumerable company of angels
        i. AMP: Countless multitudes of angels
    b. Revelation 5:11: "And the number of them was ten thousand times ten thousand, and thousands of thousands."
3. Hilton Sutton calculated that there were one hundred trillion angels
4. The angels are just waiting on your words
    a. Daniel 10:12: "Thy words were heard, and I am come for thy words."
    b. Daniel's words put the angels to work for him
5. The moment you exercise faith in your covenant, the angels go to work to minister the result of your faith back to you
    a. They are available 24 hours a day
    b. Your words put the angels to work or force them to step back
    c. Say, "Angels, go get my finances and provision and bring it back to me!"
    d. Put your prosperity angels to work!

# EAGLE MOUNTAIN
### INTERNATIONAL CHURCH

## DAYS OF PROSPERITY
**Pastor George Pearsons**

## What It Will Take to Prosper in These Times—Aggressive Faith

### Day #29

**A. Deuteronomy 28:15-68—Poverty Is an Aggressive Spirit**
1. It is part of the curse of the law
2. Examples of aggressive poverty
   a. Verse 30: You shall plant a vineyard and shall not gather the grapes
   b. Verse 38: You will carry much seed into the field and shall gather but little in, for the locust shall consume it
   c. Verse 44: The stranger shall lend to thee and thou shalt not lend to him: he shall be the head and thou shalt be the tail
3. It feeds on hopelessness and fear
4. Aggressive poverty must be countered with an aggressive faith
5. It will take a bold, aggressive faith to prosper in these times

**B. Hebrews 11:32-34—Faith Is an Aggressive Force**
1. *Faith* (GK) = PISTIS
   a. An aggressive, forward-directed force
   b. Never passive, retreating, backward or shy
2. Verses 32-34: The aggressive force of faith in action
3. 1 Samuel 17:48: David ran toward the army to meet the Philistine
4. Faith is determined, persistent and stubborn
5. Faith refuses to give up and quit—it won't let go and it will not take no for an answer

**C. Mark 11:22-24—Faith Aggressively Takes What Belongs to It**
1. Verse 24 (GK): Believe that you receive them
   a. Take with much force
   b. Seize with a grip that cannot be shaken off
2. What God has so wonderfully provided through His grace, we must lay hold of, possess and take with our faith
3. Joshua 18:3: How long are you slack to go to possess the land which the Lord God of you fathers has given you?
   a. NLT: How long are you going to wait before taking possession of the remaining land that God has given you?

      b.  MSG: How long are you going to sit around on your hands and put off taking possession of the land that God gave you?

      c.  *Possess* (HEB) = To take; to claim a territory by attacking it, seizing it, driving out the inhabitants and occupying it

5. Aggressive faith makes a demand on God's Word and takes hold on the desired result.

      a.  "Spirit of poverty, get out of my way!"

      b.  "I will either go past you or I am going to go right through you."

      c.  "Either way, I am going to aggressively take the prosperity that rightfully belongs to me in Christ Jesus!"

# EAGLE MOUNTAIN
## INTERNATIONAL CHURCH

## DAYS OF PROSPERITY
### Pastor George Pearsons

## What It Will Take to Prosper in These Times—Total Immersion

### Day #30

**A. Romans 12:1-2—Do Not Be Conformed to the World**
1. The attack on the mind is immense
2. "How are we going to make it during these times?"
3. *Conformed*—to shape like another
   a. MSG: Don't become so well-adjusted to your culture that you fit into it without even thinking
   b. PHI: Don't let the world squeeze you into its mold
4. *Transformed*—to undergo a complete change
   a. AMP: Be transformed—changed by the entire renewal of your mind by its new ideals and its new attitude
   b. GW: Change the way you think
   c. PHI: Let God remold your mind from within
5. Isaiah 26:3: "Thou wilt keep him in perfect peace, whose mind is stayed on thee: because he trusteth in thee."
   a. NLT: "You will keep in perfect peace all who trust in you, all whose thoughts are fixed on you!"
   b. *Stayed*—established, focused, totally immersed

**B. Psalm 1:1-3—The Principle of Total Immersion**
1. Verses 1-3: "Blessed is the man that walketh not in the counsel of the ungodly, nor standeth in the way of sinners, nor sitteth in the seat of the scornful. But his delight is in the law of the Lord; and in his law doth he meditate day and night. And he shall be like a tree planted by the rivers of water, that bringeth forth his fruit in his season; his leaf also shall not wither; and whatsoever he doeth shall prosper."
2. "Day and night" is total immersion in God's Word
3. Total transformation in your thinking comes from total immersion in God's Word
4. By constantly immersing yourself in God's Word, you will flush out all fear of failure and become rooted in the truth of your prosperity.
5. This is what it will take to break the lack mentality and establish a new way of thinking

## C. My Personal Total Immersion Program

1. Terri and I prayed and believed the Lord wanted us to sow our house debt free
   a. The pressure of what to do next began to consume my mind
   b. I found myself living by fear instead of faith
2. The Lord led me to do three things to totally immerse my thinking and get me back over into faith for prosperity
3. I totally immersed myself in scriptures that took my limitations off God
   a. Genesis 18:14: Is anything too hard for the Lord? NO!
   b. Numbers 11:23 (AMP): Has the Lord's hand, ability and power become short, thwarted and inadequate? NO!
   c. Matthew 19:26: With men, this is impossible. But with God, all things are possible. YES!
4. I totally immersed myself in Dr. Leroy Thompson's audio series *Money Cometh,* and Brother Copeland's audio series titled *The Laws of Prosperity.*
   a. I listened to them all the time
   b. At home, in the car, on the plane—everywhere!
5. I totally immersed myself in God's Word by locating and meditating on 21 major ways that God provides along with the total of 191 scripture references. (See document next page.)
   a. My spirit was strengthened
   b. My faith was fed
   c. My mind was renewed
   d. My life was completely transformed
   e. That is what it will take to prosper in these times

**EAGLE MOUNTAIN**

INTERNATIONAL CHURCH

## 21 Ways God Supplies

### 191 Scriptures

**1. Tithing**
- Malachi 3:10
- Leviticus 27:30
- Deuteronomy 26:1-2
- Hebrews 7:8
- Genesis 14:19-20

**2. Sowing and Reaping**
- Twice-sown seed—John 6:11
- Sowing in famine—Genesis 26:1, 12-14
- These who scatter—Proverbs 11:24-28
- Law of seedtime and harvest—Genesis 8:22; Mark 4:26-32
- Supernatural increase—Psalm 115:12-14
- Deuteronomy 16:15
- 1 Corinthians 3:6
- Psalm 62:10

**3. The Law of Multiplication**
- Multiplication—Genesis 9:7, 16:10, 17:16; 2 Corinthians 9:10
- Hundredfold return—Mark 4:20, 10:28-30; 2 Samuel 24:3
- One thousand times more—Deuteronomy 1:11; Isaiah 60:22
- Made thee a million—Ezekiel 16:7
- The Double—Isaiah 61:7; Exodus 22:7; Job 42:10

**4. Giving to the Poor**
- Proverbs 19:17
- Proverbs 28:27
- Psalm 41:1
- Matthew 19:21
- James 2:15-16
- Daniel 4:27
- The poor giving to you—1 Kings 17:9

### 5. The Ministry
- Giving to the house of the Lord—Haggai 1:7-10; 1 Chronicles 29:17, 25, 28
- Listen to the prophet—2 Chronicles 20:20
- Partnership with ministries—1 Samuel 30:24-25; 2 Kings 4:8-10
- Listen to your pastor—Psalm 23:1; Jeremiah 3:15, 23:3-4
- Increased anointing in hands of ministry—John 6:11-13
- Apostle John's greatest desire—3 John 2
- Prophet's reward—Matthew 10:41
- Righteous man's reward—Matthew 10:41

### 6. Memorial Giving
- Mark 12:41-44
- Acts 10:4
- Matthew 26:13

### 7. Our Relationship With God
- Honoring and loving God—Proverbs 3:9-10, 8:17-21
- God's pleasure in us—Psalm 35:27; Luke 12:32
- By seeking Him first—Matthew 6:33-34; Job 22:21
- Being taught by God—Isaiah 48:17

### 8. Provision Direct From the Throne
- Seed for the sower—2 Corinthians 9:10
- The hand of God—1 Chronicles 29:14-16; Numbers 11:23
- God's own ability for us—Ephesians 3:20; 2 Corinthians 9:8
- Come to the throne—Hebrews 4:16
- Daily provision—Psalm 68:19; Exodus 16:4
- His riches in glory—Philippians 4:19; Ephesians 3:16
- Your heavenly account—Philippians 4:17-20; Matthew 6:19-21
- Wisdom—Proverbs 3:13-15, 4:5-9, 24:3-4

### 9. By Creation, Re-creation and Restoration
- Creating something from faith—Genesis 1:1; Hebrews 11:1-3; Romans 4:17
- Creating something from very little—John 6:11; 1 Kings 17:13-14; 2 Kings 4:7; Luke 5:5-7
- Re-creation of a substance—John 2:7-10; Luke 3:8
- Supernatural restoration—Joel 2:25; Exodus 22:7; Proverbs 6:31

### 10. Miraculous Provision
- Debt Cancellation—Deuteronomy 15:1-2; Philemon 18-19; 1 Samuel 17:25, 22:2; 2 Kings 4:7, 6:5-6; Matthew 18:27, 6:12; Leviticus 25:10; Nehemiah 5:3-4, 11-12
- Reaping where you haven't sown—Leviticus 25:11; John 4:38
- Receiving what you didn't ask for—1 Kings 3:13
- Without money—Isaiah 55:1

## 11. Earth's Resources

- Psalm 24:1
- Psalm 33:5
- Psalm 67:5-6
- Psalm 85:11-12
- Psalm 104:24
- Deuteronomy 32:13
- Genesis 14:19
- Haggai 2:8
- Exodus 19:5
- Psalm 116:16

## 12. Hidden Treasures of Darkness

- Isaiah 45:3

## 13. Provision by Individuals

- Men—Luke 6:38; Psalms 68:29, 72:10, 112:5; Matthew 7:12; 2 Samuel 23:14-17
- Kings—Proverbs 21:1; Ezra 6:3-4, 7-8; 2 Chronicles 9:12; Esther 5:8
- Inheritance from relatives—Proverbs 19:14; 2 Corinthians 12:14

## 14. God Uses Us

- The power to get wealth—Deuteronomy 8:18; Proverbs 16:22; Genesis 24:35; Psalm 37:21-22
- Prayer of agreement—Matthew 18:18-20; 2 Kings 7:3, 5-6
- Thanksgiving—Philippians 4:6
- Work—Ephesians 4:28; 2 Thessalonians 3:10; Proverbs 6:6, 10:5, 12:11, 13:11, 14:23, 20:13; Romans 12:11
- Hand of the diligent makes rich—Proverbs 10:14, 12:24
- Thoughts of the diligent—Proverbs 21:5
- Being faithful—Luke 16:10-12, 19:17
- Being generous—1 Timothy 6:17-19
- Developing an established heart—Psalm 112:5-8
- Fasting—Matthew 6:17-18; Isaiah 58:6-8
- Confession—Proverbs 10:20, 12:18, 15:4, 18:21

## 15. Witty Inventions

- Proverbs 8:12

## 16. Simply the World's System

- The wicked and the sinner—Proverbs 13:22; Ecclesiastes 2:26; James 5:1-3
- Stolen goods returned—Exodus 22:1; Psalm 79:12; Proverbs 6:30-31, 22:22-23
- Steal it back from the enemy—Exodus 3:21-22, 12:36; 2 Chronicles 20:25; 2 Kings 7:8; Joshua 12:1, 13:1; Isaiah 53:12; 1 Samuel 30:19
- Other nations—Isaiah 61:5, 60:5

### 17. Angels
- Psalm 103:20-21
- Hebrews 1:14
- 2 Kings 6:17

### 18. Wildlife
A man shared several years ago of how he spoke to the birds to bring him money. Based upon 1 Kings 17, he said he started finding money outside around the house after he went out and hollered at the birds. They gathered around and listened to him. "People lose money every day. Go get it!"

A 15-year-old was so impressed with this story, he decided to try it. He asked the Lord for $10 for missions and God provided seed to the sower.

He went out and spoke to the birds, commanding them to put it in a tree in the backyard:

Day 1  $1.65
Day 2  $2.35
Day 3  $7
Day 4  $10

Over the next two months, he found $440 in the tree.

- 1 Kings 17:4-6
- Matthew 17:27
- Genesis 22:13-14
- Psalm 50:10

### 19. Because the Lord Needs It
- Mark 14:13-16
- Mark 11:2-3

### 20. Our Covenant Inheritance
- The Blessing of Abraham—Galatians 3:13-14
- The righteous will never beg for bread—Psalm 37:25
- Through faith and patience—Hebrews 6:12; James 1:3-5
- Our prosperous lineage—Genesis 17:1-3
- Inheritance through being a joint heir with Jesus—Galatians 3:29; Ephesians 1:10-11; Romans 8:16-17; Psalm 37:18

### 21. The Favor of God
- Exodus 11:3
- Deuteronomy 33:23
- Joshua 11:20
- 1 Samuel 16:22
- Esther 2:17
- Esther 5:8
- Esther 8:5

# EAGLE MOUNTAIN
INTERNATIONAL CHURCH

## DAYS OF PROSPERITY
**Pastor George Pearsons**

## God's Formula for Success

### Day #31

**A. Joshua 1:8 (AMP)—God's Formula for Success**
1. "This Book of the Law shall not depart out of your mouth, but you shall meditate on it day and night, that you may observe and do according to all that is written in it. For then you shall make your way prosperous, and then you shall deal wisely and have good success.
2. *Success* is defined as "the favorable outcome of something attempted."
3. Success is the result of succeeding
4. *To succeed* means to attain a desired result; to thrive, grow and prosper
5. The instructions God gave to Joshua in order to successfully possess Canaan are listed in verse 8

**B. Step No. 1—Talk God's Word**
1. Keep God's Word in your mouth at all times
2. Deuteronomy 6:6-9 (NIV): "These commandments that I give you today are to be on your hearts. Impress them on your children. Talk about them when you sit at home and when you walk along the road, when you lie down and when you get up. Tie them as symbols on your hands and bind them on your foreheads. Write them on the doorframes of your houses and on your gates."
3. Deuteronomy 11:18-21: The result of speaking the Word is that "your days may be multiplied, and the days of your children, in the land which the Lord sware unto your fathers to give them, as the days of heaven upon earth."
4. The power of your words
   a. There is no lack in this earth so great and so powerful that it cannot be turned around with words of faith
   b. The entire course of nature—your future and destiny, success and prosperity—are controlled by the words you speak
5. Hebrews 10:23: "Let us hold fast the profession [confession] of our faith without wavering…."

## C. Step No. 2—Meditate on God's Word

1. We know how to meditate
   a. Before we walked by faith, we worried all the time
   b. Worry is focusing on the dreaded outcome
2. "Meditation on the Word enlarges our capacity for faith; it transforms and expands our capacity to believe and receive." —Kenneth Copeland
3. Meditation on God's Word is fixing your mind and setting your heart on the desired result
4. Psalm 1:1-3: "Blessed is the man that walketh not in the counsel of the ungodly, nor standeth in the way of sinners, nor sitteth in the seat of the scornful. But his delight is in the law of the Lord; and in his law doth he meditate day and night. And he shall be like a tree planted by the rivers of water, that bringeth forth his fruit in his season; his leaf also shall not wither; and whatsoever he doeth shall prosper."
5. How to meditate God's Word
   a. Apply the Word to you personally
   b. Allow the Holy Spirit to make the Word a reality in your heart
   c. Carefully ponder how this Word applies to your life
   d. Dwell on how the Word changes your situation
   e. Place yourself in agreement with what the Word says about you
   f. See yourself as God sees you
   g. Realize the integrity in God's Word

## D. Step No. 3—Act on the Word

1. It is easy to act on God's Word if you have been speaking the Word and meditating on the Word
2. Luke 6:47-49: Same storm—different results
   a. Verse 47: "Whosoever cometh to me, and heareth my sayings, and doeth them, I will show you to whom he is like."
   b. Verse 48: "He is like a man which built an house and digged deep, and laid the foundation on a rock: and when the flood arose, the stream beat vehemently upon that house, and could not shake it: for it was founded upon a rock."
   c. Verse 49: "But he that heareth and doeth not, is like a man that without a foundation built an house upon the earth; against which the stream did beat vehemently, and immediately it fell; and the ruin of that house was great."
3. James 1:22: Decide: I don't just hear the Word—I am a doer of that Word
4. Put the formula together
   a. Find out what God's Word says about your financial situation.
   b. Speak that Word in faith, believing for the desired result
   c. Meditate upon it until the Word becomes greater on the inside then the lack on the outside
   d. Then, fearlessly act on what you see in the Word, knowing that no word from God is void or without power
5. The result is that you will make your way prosperous, deal wisely in the affairs of life and have good success

# EAGLE MOUNTAIN
### INTERNATIONAL CHURCH

## DAYS OF PROSPERITY
### Pastor George Pearsons

## How to Apply for a Heavenly Grant

### Day #32

**A. From *The Laws of Prosperity* CD Series**
1. During the very early years of Kenneth and Gloria's ministry, A.W. Copeland, Kenneth's father, was the business administrator and only employee
2. He came to Kenneth one day and said, "Do you have any idea how much money it takes to operate this ministry?"
3. Brother Copeland replied, "No, and I don't want to know!"
4. His father said, "I think you ought to pray about it. We have grown so much in the last 90 days that I don't think you have any idea what it costs to run this."
5. He laid a piece of paper on Kenneth's desk with a figure on it and then walked away.
   a. Kenneth picked up the paper, looked at it and "almost choked"!
   b. He then said to himself, "Looks like I should do something about this."

**B. The Lord Began to Speak**
1. "Boy, don't you start that. You know better than that."
2. "You know who your Source of supply is."
3. "You get over there on your knees and you get it that way!"
4. As Brother Copeland began to pray, the Lord told him to look up two scriptures in *The Amplified Bible*
   a. John 16:23: "And when that time comes, you will ask nothing of Me [you will need to ask Me no questions]. I assure you, most solemnly I tell you, that My Father will grant you whatever you ask in My Name."
   b. Mark 11:24: "For this reason I am telling you, whatever you ask for in prayer, believe (trust and be confident) that it is granted to you, and you will [get it]."
5. *Grant* defined
   a. A sum of money provided by a government, local authority or public fund to finance educational study, overseas aid, building repairs, etc.
   b. There are students able to attend college because of a grant
   c. To grant—to give, bestow or confer
   d. A heavenly grant comes from another Source

### C. How to Apply for a Heavenly Grant

1. Brother Copland took the piece of paper his dad gave to him and wrote on it
2. "According to John 16:23 (AMP), I submit this request in the Name of Jesus: I lay claim of my heavenly grant of $_____ every 30 days."
3. "According to Mark 11:24 (AMP), I am confident that whatever I ask in prayer, it is granted to me. I believe I receive my grant in Jesus' Name."
4. From that moment on, the finances came in
5. That was 40 years ago—and the bills are still paid in full!

### D. A Sample Request for a Heavenly Grant

*Be it known this day, _____, we receive a heavenly grant in the amount of $_____. Father, in the Name of Jesus, we come boldly to the throne of grace, and present Your Word.*

*According to John 16:23 (AMP), Jesus said, "I assure you, most solemnly I tell you, that My Father will grant you whatever you ask in My Name."*

*Jesus, You said in Mark 11:24 (AMP), "Whatever you ask for in prayer, believe (trust and be confident) that it is granted to you, and you will [get it]."*

*Your Word states in Luke 6:38, "Give, and it shall be given unto you; good measure, pressed down, and shaken together, and running over, shall men give unto your bosom." In accordance to Your Word, we give, we sow seed, in order to set this spiritual law to work on our behalf.*

*According to Matthew 18:18, we bind Satan and all his forces, and render them helpless and unable to operate. They will not hinder our grant.*

*According to Hebrews 1:13 and 14, we loose the ministering spirits and charge them to go forth and cause our grant to come into our hands.*

*Jesus, You said in Matthew 18:19, "Again I say until you, That if two of you shall agree on earth as touching any thing that they shall ask, it shall be done for them of My Father which is in heaven."*

*Therefore, we set ourselves in agreement, and we believe we receive now, and we praise You for it.*

**EAGLE MOUNTAIN**

INTERNATIONAL CHURCH

## DAYS OF PROSPERITY
**Pastor George Pearsons**

## You Can Live Debt Free—Part 1

### Day #33

**A. Matthew 6:33—Seek First the Kingdom of God**

1. "Seek ye first the kingdom of God, and his righteousness; and all these things shall be added unto you."

2. AMP: "But seek, aim at and strive after first of all His kingdom and His righteousness, His way of doing and being right, and then all these things taken together will be given you besides."

3. How do we seek first the kingdom? We give God's Word first place and final authority in our lives.

4. Commit yourself to obey whatever you see in the Word

5. From *God's Will Is Prosperity* by Gloria Copeland

   a. "Kenneth and I made that very commitment (the commitment to obey whatever they saw in the Word) years ago when we first began to find out how faith works. We agreed then that we would do whatever we saw in God's Word. Without even knowing it, we had placed ourselves in position to receive great financial blessings."

   b. "Our desire was to please God: we were committed to His Word. We didn't know how to believe God for material things. We didn't even know that the instructions in God's Word would always work to our advantage—even in this life."

   c. "When we first learned that God would meet our needs, we were living in Tulsa, Oklahoma, where Kenneth was enrolled in Oral Roberts University. We desired to please God with all of our hearts, and we had moved out in what little faith we knew."

   d. "Financially, times were hard. I really think that we were supernaturally in debt! No matter how hard we tried, we couldn't get out of debt; we just seemed to get in deeper and deeper. Borrowed money was our source. After we paid the bills, there was no money left for anything else."

   e. "Old obligations were left unpaid, and there was threat of a lawsuit. I can remember standing in the checkout line at the grocery store, praying in the spirit, and believing God that I had enough money to pay for the groceries in my basket. Whatever I had in my purse at the time was all we had!"

f. "We didn't know then what we know now about operating in the laws of prosperity. We were just beginning to learn about the integrity of the Word: that you can depend on God's Word in the same way you depend on the word of a doctor, a lawyer or your very best friend."

g. "We know that the Word of God never fails. We committed to do whatever we saw in the Word, no matter what it was."

h. "Then we saw Romans 13:8...."

**B. Romans 13:8—"Owe no man any thing but to love one another."**
1. "Surely God didn't mean that!"
2. "That scripture must mean something else!"
3. AMP: "Keep out of debt and owe no man anything, except to love one another."
4. "It looked impossible to do anything without borrowing money. We had never considered paying cash for a car. We had never bought furniture. How would we ever have anything? The material possession I wanted most in the world was a home. Pay cash for a house? You must be kidding! Satan would say, 'You will never get it.' We actually did not know that we could receive all these things with our faith."
5. "We had a choice, but not a good one as far as we could tell. We had said, 'We are taking God's Word literally and whatever we see in it, that is what we will do.' But when we made that commitment, we did not know the Bible said, 'Keep out of debt.'"

**C. From *The Laws of Prosperity* by Kenneth Copeland**
1. "When Gloria and I first began to put the things we were learning into practice, we had nothing around us but problems. I had returned to college at the age of 30 and from there, God called us into a full-time ministry in His service."
2. "We were deeply in debt and lived in surroundings that were very poor. The job God called me to do required that I travel extensively preaching and teaching His Word, but our car was worn out. We had less than nothing. We were thousands of dollars in debt."
3. "God used His Word to set the standards by which we would operate. It had to be by faith or not at all. We made commitments that seemed so hard. We declared that we would never ask any man for anything including money and places to minister."
4. "We pledged ourselves and this ministry to Romans 13:8 that we would never borrow one cent. We would tell our needs only to God and expect what He was teaching us to produce. We prayed, confessed our faith and stood on God's Word when every circumstance spelled absolute doom. God's Word worked!"
5. "Things began to happen for us instead of to us. We began to grow. In eleven months, we were free from debt."

**D. Make a Quality Decision to Live Debt Free**
1. A quality decision
   a. It forever settles the issue
   b. It is a decision of no retreat and no return
   c. It is a memorial that settles all future decisions

2. "The very moment you make the quality decision to live debt free, God sees you debt free."
3. Settle forever
   a. God is my Source—not people
   b. I am not limited to a salary
   c. It is God's will for me to live debt free

# EAGLE MOUNTAIN
### INTERNATIONAL CHURCH

## DAYS OF PROSPERITY
**Pastor George Pearsons**

## You Can Live Debt Free—Part 2

### Day #34

**A. Matthew 6:33—Seek First the Kingdom of God**
 1. "Seek ye first the kingdom of God, and his righteousness; and all these things shall be added unto you."
 2. AMP: "But seek (aim at and strive after) first of all His kingdom and His righteousness (His way of doing and being right), and then all these things taken together will be given you besides."
 3. Kenneth and Gloria Copeland committed themselves to seek the kingdom by:
     a. Giving God's Word first place
     b. Making God's Word final authority
     c. Committing to obey whatever they saw in the Word
 4. Financial times were hard and they were in debt
 5. And then they saw Romans 13:8

**B. Romans 13:8—"Owe no man any thing but to love one another."**
 1. AMP: "Keep out of debt and owe no man anything, except to love one another."
 2. It looked impossible to do, but they did it
 3. They made a quality decision to live debt free
 4. A quality decision forever settles the issue, is a decision of no retreat and is a memorial that settles all future decision
 5. They settled forever that God was their Source, they were not limited and it was God's will for them to live debt free

**C. What Kenneth and Gloria Copeland Did to Live Debt Free**
—From *God's Will Is Prosperity* by Gloria Copeland
 1. "We stopped using our charge accounts and began to believe God to get out of debt."
     a. "Everything we owned was 'buy now, pay later.'"
     b. "Sometimes it was much later!"
 2. "We set our affections on God's Word."
     a. "We were determined to walk according to what we saw in the Word."
     b. "Things didn't come to us in one day. We had to build the Word of God into our spirits and walk in what we knew. We would get some of the Word in us and walk in it; get more Word in us and walk in that; get more Word in us and

walk in that. We were involved in the Word almost every waking hour. Television was not interesting to us. Even the world events could not hold our attention."

    c. "We were committed to the Word regardless and were not willing to borrow money."

3. "We devoted ourselves to God's Word literally day and night."

    a. Joshua 1:8 (AMP): "This book of the law shall not depart out of your mouth, but you shall meditate on it day and night, that you may observe and do according to all that is written in it. For then you shall make your way prosperous, and then you shall deal wisely and have good success.

4. "It was 11 months from the time that we first decided to believe God to get out of debt until that goal was achieved. During those 11 months, we stood fast on what we knew from God's Word."

5. From *The Laws of Prosperity* by Kenneth Copeland

    a. "We figured out how much we owed. I got my checkbook and wrote out the checks that would pay these debts. We laid hands on them and prayed according to Romans 13:8."

    b. "Father, in the Name of Jesus, I am putting these checks in this desk drawer and am believing You to get us out of this mess. I am looking to You for the money to pay all these debts, in the Name of Jesus."

    c. "I did not mail those checks until the money was in the bank!"

    d. "We figured to the last penny how much it would take to operate our household abundantly, even allowing for unexpected things. We wrote it down and prayed over it in the Name of Jesus."

    e. "I made up my mind to be single-minded from that day forward. In less than 12 months from that day, we did not owe anything!"

# EAGLE MOUNTAIN
### INTERNATIONAL CHURCH

## DAYS OF PROSPERITY
**Pastor George Pearsons**

## The Grace of Giving

### Day #35

**A. 2 Corinthians 8:7—The Grace of Giving**
1. "Therefore, as ye abound in every thing, in faith, in utterance, and knowledge, and in all diligence, and in your love to us, see that ye abound in this grace also."
2. "It grieves Me when the church takes offerings. I said to worship Me. Don't take from the people, but let them bring it and worship Me. Then they will see the fruit of their giving." —word from the Lord to Lynne Hammond
3. "We must learn to excel at the grace of giving." —Gloria Copeland

**B. 2 Corinthians 9:6—Give Willingly**
1. AMP: "Remember this: he who sows sparingly and grudgingly will also reap sparingly and grudgingly, and he who sows generously [that blessings may come to someone] will also reap generously and with blessings."
   a. It is not the amount
   b. Is the attitude
2. Exodus 35:4-5: "This is the thing which the Lord commanded, saying, Take ye from among you an offering unto the Lord: whosoever is of a willing heart, let him bring it."
3. Mark 12:41-44 (NLT): "…They gave a tiny part of their surplus [grudgingly], but she, poor as she is, has given everything she had to live on [willingly and bountifully]."

**C. 2 Corinthians 9:7—Give from the Heart**
1. AMP: "Let each one [give] as he has made up his own mind and purposed in his heart."
2. JBP: "Let everyone give as his heart tells him."
3. Exodus 35:20-21: "And all the congregation of the children of Israel departed from the presence of Moses. And they came, every one whose heart stirred him up, and every one whom his spirit made willing, and they brought the Lord's offering to the work of the tabernacle."
   a. *Stirred* (HEB) = Moved, inspired, directed, led

**D. 2 Corinthians 9:7—Give Cheerfully**

1. "Not grudgingly, or of necessity: for God loveth a cheerful giver."

2. AMP: "Not reluctantly or sorrowfully or under compulsion, for God loves a cheerful (joyous, "prompt to do it") giver [whose heart is in his giving]."

3. *Cheerful* (GK) HILAROS = hilarious and joyful

**E. 2 Corinthians 9:8—The Result of Excelling at the Grace of Giving**

1. "And God is able to make all grace abound toward you; that ye, always having all sufficiency in all things, may abound to every good work."

2. AMP: "God is able to make all grace (every favor and earthly blessing) come to you in abundance, so that you may always and under all circumstances and whatever the need be self-sufficient [possessing enough to require no aid or support and furnished in abundance for every good work and charitable donation]."

3. NLT: "And God will generously provide all you need. Then you will always have everything you need and plenty left to share with others."

## DAYS OF PROSPERITY
**Pastor George Pearsons**

## The God of the Breakthrough Will Visit Your House

### Day #36

**A. Jerry Savelle Experienced a Visitation from the Lord in February 2004**
1. He had just arrived in Liberty, Texas, to preach
2. He checked into the hotel and was going to rest before the service
3. The Lord visited Brother Jerry and spoke a word to him
4. "My people are overwhelmed by financial attacks. I want you to tell them that the God of the breakthrough will visit their home. Tell them that they know Me as Savior, Redeemer and soon-coming King—but they don't know Me as the God of the breakthrough. If they did, they wouldn't be so quick to give up. I want you to show them how to position themselves to receive the God of the breakthrough into their home."
5. The Lord then took him to 1 Kings 17:8-16 and gave him three keys that will produce supernatural breakthrough

**B. The Three Keys That Will Produce Supernatural Breakthrough**
1. Key No. 1—A supernatural breakthrough requires a prophetic word from God
    a. A *rhema* word—a specific word relevant for right now
    b. The prophet told the woman if she did what he said to do, she would experience a breakthrough
        i. Verse 13: Make me a cake first
    c. Psalm 85:8: "I will hear what God the Lord will speak: for he will speak peace unto his people, and to his saints."
        i. AMP: "I will listen with expectancy to what God the Lord will say."
        ii. Set time aside to hear the plan of God for your breakthrough
2. Key No. 2—A supernatural breakthrough requires a willingness to receive and obey the prophetic word
    a. The widow went and did what the prophet told her to do
    b. Isaiah 1:19 If you be willing and obedient, you will eat the good of the land
3. Key No. 3—A supernatural breakthrough requires the sowing of a significant seed
    a. A significant seed is a seed that is valuable to you

b. Verses 15-16: "She went and did according to the saying of Elijah: and she, and he, and her house, did eat many days [HEB—a full year]. The barrel of meal wasted not, neither did the cruse of oil fail."

c. As a result of the significant seed, God turned her "have not" into "plenty."
   i. Mark 12:41-44—The widow's mite
   ii. While in the hospital, Oral Roberts told Evelyn to sow the biggest seed possible. The result was the lengthening of his years and ministry.

## C. What to Expect When You Do These Three Keys

1. Expect God to bring you out of bondage
   a. Genesis 50:24: "Joseph said unto his brethren, I die: and God will surely visit you, and bring you out of this land unto the land which he sware to Abraham, to Isaac, and to Jacob."
2. Expect God to bless you with His favor like never before
   a. Job 10:12: "Thou hast granted me life and favour, and thy visitation hath preserved my spirit."
3. Expect God to bring supernatural increase to your house
   a. Psalm 65:9: "You visitest the earth and waterest it: you greatly enrichest it with the river of God which is full of water: thou preparest them corn, when thou hast so provided for it."

## D. The God of Your Breakthrough

1. John 14:6: Jesus said, "I am the way."
2. Jesus says, "I have made a way for you where there is no way."
3. 1 Chronicles 14:11: "So they came up to Baalperazim; and David smote [the Philistines] there. Then David said, God has broken in upon mine enemies by mine hand like the breaking forth of waters: therefore they call the name of that place Baalperazim."
4. AMP: "Therefore they called the name of that place Baal-perazim [Lord of breaking through]."
5. "The depth of your praise will determine the magnitude of your harvest."
   —Jerry Savelle

# EAGLE MOUNTAIN
INTERNATIONAL CHURCH

## DAYS OF PROSPERITY
**Pastor George Pearsons**

## Sow Your Way Out of Financial Pressure

### Day #37

A. **Ecclesiastes 11:4**—"He that observeth the wind shall not sow; and he that regardeth the clouds shall not reap."
   1. When money gets tight and the pressure is on, it is always a temptation to cut down on your giving
   2. It seems like the "logical" thing to do
   3. Don't do that!
   4. You cut off the flow of God's financial blessings just when you need it the most
   5. The right way to defeat an attack of lack is to sow your way out

B. **"Lord, I Need $1 Million!"**
   1. Many years ago, KCM was behind financially
   2. Kenneth and Gloria had seen God provide over and over
   3. This was a tough one—all the prayers and the faith that had brought them previous victory didn't seem to get the job done
   4. By the end of the year, the deficit was $1 million
   5. Kenneth went before the Lord
      a. "Lord, I need $1 million."
      b. "The Lord replied, 'No you don't!'"
      c. "When you talk to the Lord about your need, He will talk to you about sowing seed." —Jerry Savelle

C. **Proverbs 11:24 (NLT)—"Give freely and become more wealthy; be stingy and lose everything."**
   1. The Lord told Kenneth that the red ink on the books was not the only thing wrong
   2. There was a bigger problem behind it
   3. He showed Kenneth that he needed to start giving 10 percent of the ministry's income into ministering to the poor
   4. How do you solve a deficit by giving?
   5. As KCM began to sow the 10 percent, the million dollar deficit began to disappear

# DAYS OF PROSPERITY
**Pastor George Pearsons**

## Don't Forget to Factor the Anointing

### Day #38

**A. Ephesians 2:12-13—The Missing Element**
1. People experience financial demands during challenging times
2. They are trying to figure out how to supply their own need
3. Under the pressure, they forget to include the key element that would completely alter their financial condition
4. Ephesians 2:12-13: "Ye were without Christ, being aliens from the commonwealth of Israel, and strangers from the covenants of promise, having no hope, and without God in the world: But now in Christ Jesus, ye who sometimes were far off are made nigh by the blood of Christ."
5. They forget about the Anointed One and His Anointing

**B. Luke 4:18—19—The Purpose of the Anointing**
1. Verses 18-19: "The spirit of the Lord is upon me because He hath anointed me to preach the gospel to the poor; He hath sent me to heal the brokenhearted, to preach deliverance to the captives, and recovering of sight to the blind, to set at liberty them that are bruised, to preach the acceptable year of the Lord."
2. The acceptable year of the Lord
    a. The year of Jubilee
    b. The year when all debts were canceled and released
    c. AMP: "The day when salvation and the free favors of God profusely abound."
3. Verse 21: "This day is this scripture fulfilled in your ears"—right now!
4. Isaiah 10:27: "It shall come to pass in that day, that his burden shall be taken away from off thy shoulder and his yoke from off thy neck, and the yoke shall be destroyed because of the anointing."
    a. *Burden*—a heavy load carried with great difficulty; to be weighed down
    b. *Yoke*—agency of oppression, slavery and servitude
        i. A symbol of subjection
        ii. Roman times—a defeated army was made to "walk under the yoke" as a symbol of defeat and humiliation
5. The anointing for prosperity
    a. *To anoint*—is God's provision poured over, smeared on and rubbed into our financial lives

      b. It is the burden-removing, yoke-destroying power of God
         i. The power of God that removes the burden of lack
         ii. The power of God that destroys the yoke of debt
      c. It is the power of God on our lives doing only what God can do
      d. It is God's "super" abundance added to our "natural" situation

## C. Don't Forget to Factor the Anointing!
1. Factor—to include as an essential element
2. The anointing will make a way where there is no way
3. The anointing will accelerate the increase of your storehouses
4. The anointing will wipe out outstanding debts
5. The anointing of God will reveal the wisdom you need to thrive and not just survive in these times

You cannot prosper in God
without Jesus' anointing
His Anointing Does Not Work
on The unfaithful or sinful

Brother Copeland handed this note to me while Gloria was preaching at EMIC on January 8, 1995. Her topic that evening was "Foundation for Prosperity."

# EAGLE MOUNTAIN
### INTERNATIONAL CHURCH

## DAYS OF PROSPERITY
**Pastor George Pearsons**

## Prosperity and Praise

### Day #39

*"The depth of your praise will determine the magnitude of your harvest."*
*—Jerry Savelle*

**A. Galatians 6:9**—"Let us not be weary in well doing: for in due season we shall reap, if we faint not."
1. AMP: "Let us not lose heart and grow weary and faint in acting nobly and doing right, for in due time and at the appointed season we shall reap, if we do not loosen and relax our courage and faint."
2. Many lose heart and complain that their sowing is not working
   a. How foolish it would be for a farmer to dig up his seed the day after it was planted because he didn't see results
   b. It is just as foolish for a believer to dig up his seed because he didn't see results
3. What do we do between the time we sow our seed and reap our harvest?
4. There is one key factor that will bring your seed all the way through to full harvest
5. "The depth of your praise will determine the magnitude of your harvest."
   —Jerry Savelle

**B. The Power of Praise**
1. What praise does for us
   a. Praise gives voice to our faith
   b. Praise is the expression of utmost confidence in God's Word
   c. Praise helps things "move along."
2. Psalm 8:2: "Out of the mouth of babes and sucklings hast thou ordained [praise] because of thine enemies, that thou mightest still enemy and the avenger."
   a. Praise stops the enemy of lack
3. Psalm 9:1-3: "I will praise thee, O Lord, with my whole heart; I will show forth all thy marvellous works. I will be glad and rejoice in thee: I will sing praise to thy name, O thou most High. When mine enemies are turned back, they shall fall and perish at thy presence."
   a. Praise pushes back lack
   b. Praise causes lack to fall and perish

       c. Praise brings the presence of God on the scene
    4. Psalm 22:3: "But thou art holy, O thou that inhabitest the praises of Israel."
       a. The Supernatural Provider inhabits our praise
    5. Habakkuk 3:17-19: "Although the fig tree shall not blossom, neither shall fruit be in the vines; the labour of the olive shall fail, and the fields shall yield no meat; the flock shall be cut off from the fold, and there shall be no herd in the stalls: Yet I will rejoice in the Lord, I will joy in the God of my salvation. The Lord God is my strength, and he will make my feet like hinds' feet, and he will make me to walk upon mine high places."
       a. HEB: "I will joy in the God of my prosperity and deliverance."
       b. HEB: "The Lord God is my wealth."

**C. Psalm 67:5-7**—"Let the people praise thee, O God; let all the people praise thee. Then shall the earth yield her increase; and God, even our own God, shall bless us. God shall bless us; and all the ends of the earth shall fear Him."
    1. Increase comes from praise
    2. Verse 7 (MSG): "You mark us with blessing."
    3. Testimony from a family who praises God
       a. An EMIC family travels from rural Oklahoma to church every Sunday
       b. Several years ago, they brought to me a huge watermelon from their garden
       c. It was during a severe dry season and their garden was the only one producing.
       d. This year, they decided to let their land rest
       e. The land yielded a full harvest in spite of the fact that they did not even sow—they just kept praising God!!

**DAYS OF PROSPERITY**
**Pastor George Pearsons**

## Take It!

### Day #40

A. **Joshua 18:1-3**—"How long are ye slack to go to posses the land, which the Lord God of your fathers hath given you?"
1. NLT: "How long are you going to wait before taking possession of the remaining land the Lord, the God of your ancestors, has given to you?"
2. GDN: "How long are you going to wait before you go in and take the land?"
3. MSG: "How long are you going to sit around on your hands, putting off taking possession of the land that God, the God of your ancestors has given you?"
4. *Slack* (HEB)
   a. Postpone, put off and waste time
   b. Slow, sluggish and lazy
5. How long are you going to put off and be spiritually lazy taking what is yours in Christ?

B. **Mark 11:22-24—Faith Takes!**
1. *Faith* (GK) PISTIS = full persuasion and conviction
2. Faith is never passive, retreating or backward
   a. Hebrews 10:38-39: "The just shall live by faith: but if any man draw back, my soul shall have no pleasure in him. But we are not of them who draw back unto perdition; but of them that believe to the saving of the soul."
3. Faith is an aggressive force
   a. Faith is always moving forward
   b. Faith continually reaches for its goal
   c. Hebrews 11:33: Who through faith they subdued, possessed and conquered kingdoms
4. Mark 11:24: "Believe that ye receive them, and ye shall have them."
   a. (GK) Take it with much force
   b. (GK) Get hold of
   c. (GK) Seize with a grip which cannot be shaken off
5. Matthew 11:12: "From the days of John the Baptist until now the kingdom of heaven suffereth violence, and the violent take it by force."
   a. We take what is ours with the force of faith

      b. To take by force (GK) HARPADZO
         i. Harpoon
         ii. To pull
         iii. "Moby Dick" says it all!

**C. Nehemiah 9:21-25—Go In and Take the Land!**
1. Verse 24: "So the children went in and possessed the land."
    a. They went in and took it
2. Verse 25: "And they took strong cities, and a fat [rich, plenteous and wealthy] land, and possessed houses full of all goods, wells digged, vineyards, and oliveyards, and fruit trees in abundance."
3. Verse 25: "So they did eat, and were filled, and became fat [rich, plenteous and wealthy], and delighted themselves in thy great goodness."
4. Jesus paid the price for us to walk in the blessing of Abraham.
5. Take it in Jesus' Name!!

## DAYS OF PROSPERITY
**Pastor George Pearsons**

## Living in Days of Prosperity

### Day #41

**A. Psalm 25:12-13—Days of Prosperity**
1. NIV: "Who, then, are those who fear the Lord? He will instruct them in the ways they should choose. They will spend their days in prosperity, and their descendants will inherit the land."
2. NLT: "They will live in prosperity."
3. KJV: "His soul shall dwell at ease."
   a. *Ease* (HEB) = prosperity, bountiful wealth and good in the widest possible sense

**B. Job 36:11—Years of Pleasures**
1. "If they obey and serve him, they shall spend their days in prosperity and their years in pleasures."
2. *Pleasures* (HEB): Your years will be delightful, pleasant and sweet
3. AMP: Years in pleasantness and joy
4. NLT: "If they listen and obey God, they will be blessed with prosperity throughout their lives. All their years will be pleasant."
5. Isaiah 1:19: "If ye be willing and obedient, ye shall eat the good of the land."
   a. MSG: "If you'll willingly obey, you'll feast like kings."

**C. Expect Prosperity Every Day for the Rest of Your Life**
1. Psalm 68:19: "Blessed be the Lord, who daily loadeth us with benefits, even the God of our salvation."
   a. BBE: "[He] is our support day by day."
   b. DRB: "He will make our journey prosperous."
2. Matthew 6:11: "Give us this day our daily bread."
   a. DRB: "Give us this day our supersubstantial bread."
3. Job 36:11 (NIV): "If they obey and serve him, they will spend the rest of their days in prosperity and their years in contentment."

a. *Spend* (HEB) = complete, live out, accomplish and end his days in prosperity
b. Psalm 92:12-14: "The righteous shall flourish like the palm tree: he shall grow like a cedar in Lebanon. Those that be planted in the house of the Lord shall flourish in the courts of our God. They shall still bring forth fruit in old age; they shall be fat and flourishing."

# EAGLE MOUNTAIN
### INTERNATIONAL CHURCH

## DAYS OF PROSPERITY
### Pastor George Pearsons

## We Lack Nothing—Part 1

### Day #42

**A. Luke 22:35—Did You Lack Anything?**
 1. GW: "Then Jesus said to them, 'When I sent you out without a wallet, traveling bag, or sandals, you didn't lack anything, did you?' 'Not a thing!' they answered."
 2. *Lack* (GK) = fall short, come behind, be destitute, be deficient
 3. When we believe God and stand on His Word, we will not fall short, come behind, be destitute or be deficient in anything

**B. 1 Thessalonians 4:11-12—That You May Have Lack of Nothing**
 1. "Study to be quiet, and to do your own business, and to work with your own hands, as we commanded you; that ye may walk honestly toward them that are without, and that you may have lack of nothing."
 2. AMP: "Make it your ambition and definitely endeavor to live quietly and peacefully, to mind your own affairs, and to work with your hands, as we charged you, so that you may bear yourselves becomingly and be correct and honorable and command the respect of the outside world, being dependent on nobody [self-supporting] and having need of nothing."
 3. GNB: "In this way you will win the respect of those who are not believers, and you will not have to depend on anyone for what you need."

**C. James 1:2-6—Perfect and Entire, Wanting Nothing**
 1. "Count it all joy when ye fall into divers temptations; knowing this, that the trying of your faith worketh patience. But let patience have her perfect work, that ye may be perfect and entire, wanting nothing. If any of you lack wisdom, let him ask of God, that giveth to all men liberally and upbraideth not; and it shall be given him. But let him ask in faith, nothing wavering."
 2. Various "wanting nothing" translations
     a. ASV: Lacking in nothing
     b. BBE: Needing nothing
     c. CEV: Not lacking in anything
     d. DRB: Failing in nothing
     e. GW: You won't need anything
     f. MSG: Not deficient in any way
 3. If any of you lacks provision, let him ask of God, who gives to all men liberally

## EAGLE MOUNTAIN
INTERNATIONAL CHURCH

## DAYS OF PROSPERITY
**Pastor George Pearsons**

## We Lack Nothing—Part 2

### Day #43

**A. Luke 22:35—Did You Lack Anything?**
1. CEV: "Jesus asked his disciples, 'When I sent you out without a moneybag or a traveling bag or sandals, did you need anything?' 'No!' they answered."
2. The disciples grew in their revelation of God's provision
3. Verse 36 (AMP): "But now let him who has a purse take it, and also [his provision] bag; and let him that has no sword sell his mantle and buy a sword."

**B. Jeremiah 23:4—Neither Shall They be Lacking**
1. "I will set up shepherds over them which shall feed them: and they shall fear no more, nor be dismayed, neither shall they be lacking."
2. It is the responsibility of the ministers to teach their congregations the laws that govern supernatural abundance and provision in these economic times so that their congregations do not lack anything
3. Luke 4:18: "The Spirit of the Lord is upon me, because he hath anointed me to preach the gospel to the poor."
    a. The poor don't have to be poor anymore
    b. They don't have to lack anything

**C. 2 Corinthians 9:8—Furnished in Abundance**
1. AMP: "God is able to make all grace (every favor and earthly blessing) come to you in abundance, so that you may always and under all circumstances and whatever the need be self-sufficient [possessing enough to require no aid or support and furnished in abundance for every good work and charitable donation]."
    a. KJV: Having all sufficiency
    b. BBE: Having enough of all things
    c. RSV: You may always have enough of everything
2. Psalm 34:9-10: "Fear the Lord, ye his saints: for there is no want to them that fear him. The young lions do lack, and suffer hunger: but they that seek the Lord [AMP—on the authority of His Word] shall not want any good thing."

3. Psalm 37:25: "I have been young, and now am old; yet have I not seen the righteous forsaken, nor his seed begging bread."
4. Psalm 84:11: "For the Lord God is a sun and shield: the Lord will give grace and glory: no good thing will He withhold from them that walk uprightly."
5. James 1:17 (AMP): "Every good gift and every perfect (free, large, full) gift is from above; it comes down from the Father of all [that gives] light."

# EAGLE MOUNTAIN
INTERNATIONAL CHURCH

## DAYS OF PROSPERITY
**Pastor George Pearsons**

## Now Is Not the Time to Quit Tithing—Part 1

### Day #44

**A. Recent Survey Concerning the Economy's Effect on Giving**
1. "The economy has changed many aspects of American life. A new research study explores how the charitable landscape has changed over the last two and a half years. The study examines how many Americans have been affected by the economic downturn, how this has influenced their donations and their outlook on economic recovery."
2. "Church giving has declined since the beginning of this year:
   a. 24% have stopped all giving to churches.
   b. 17% have decreased their giving by 20% or less.
   c. 7% have lessened their donations by 20% to 45%.
   d. 17% have reduced their giving by half.
   e. 12% have decreased their giving by more than half."
3. "The study revealed that the number of people who are tithing has also dropped.
   a. The practice of tithing—donating at least 10% of one's income to churches or other charities—has been relatively stable over the past decade, hovering between 5% and 7%.
   b. Currently, the national tithing rate is down to 4% of the adult population."
4. "It is true that many Americans are living on less due to salary reductions, furloughs, loss of jobs or the inability to get a position that matched a previous salary. These are difficult circumstances for anyone to face and could have a legitimate influence on donations."
5. "However, most of the survey indicators focus less on the amount of dollars donated and more on the underlying attitudes and generosity of Americans. Most Americans think of their giving as secondary to their survival. Yet, from a biblical perspective, generosity should be part of the Christian's fundamental response to the downturn."

**"Now is not the time to quit tithing!"**

## B. Malachi 3:10-12—Bring Ye All the Tithes
1. The tithe is the 10 percent of all our income
2. Tithing is the faith action by which we bring the 10 percent to Jesus—the High Priest of the tithe
3. The tithe goes to where we are fed so that we can continue to be fed
4. God uses the 10 percent to reinvest into our spiritual welfare and benefit
5. Tithing is the only place in the Bible where God says, "Prove Me."

## C. Leviticus 27:30, 32—The Tithe Belongs to God
1. Verse 30: All the tithe is holy unto the Lord
2. Verse 32: "The tenth shall be holy unto the Lord."
3. *Holy* (HEB) = separated from, consecrated to
4. We are to worship God with our tithe
5. The tithe gives God the opportunity to fulfill His covenant and protect the other 90 percent
   a. The tithe places us under warranty
   b. Everything is covered

## D. A.W. Copeland's Testimony About Tithing During the Great Depression
From the August 1980 *Believer's Voice of Victory* Magazine

In looking back over the years, more specifically the years of the Depression, Vinita and I can see how God really took care of us. He kept me in jobs when there were no jobs. Because of our decision to live for Him, He made sure that our every need was met.

Even though the Depression years were hard for many, we now see how the Lord met our needs and kept us. The Depression never did have any devastating effect on our lives because we knew the Lord.

One of the real keys that kept us going was the fact that we were tithing. Whether we were working for a salary or on the farm, we tithed. When I made Jesus the Lord of my life, I also made Him Lord over everything I had.

We never missed a payment on our home or any of the cars we owned. I just kept on working and we just kept on tithing. We never lacked anything.

EAGLE MOUNTAIN

INTERNATIONAL CHURCH

## DAYS OF PROSPERITY
**Pastor George Pearsons**

## Now Is Not the Time to Quit Tithing—Part 2

**Day #45**

**A. Now Is Not the Time to Quit Tithing**
1. Recent survey reports that giving and tithing is down
2. Malachi 3:8-12—The tithe is the 10 percent of our income and tithing is the process of giving it by faith
3. The tithe goes to where we are spiritually fed so we can continue to be fed
4. Leviticus 27:30, 32—The tithe belongs to God and He reinvests it for our benefit
5. "One of the real keys that kept us going was the fact that we were tithing. We never missed a payment. I just kept on working and we just kept on tithing. We never lacked anything." —A.W. Copeland, referring to tithing during the Great Depression

**B. Deuteronomy 26:1-15—The Proper Handling of the Tithe**
1. Tithing is the faith action that sets the covenant of blessing in motion that opens the windows of heaven
2. Tithing is done with words of faith, prayerfully and by love
3. Hebrews 3:1, 7:8—Jesus is the High Priest of the tithe
4. Jesus takes your tithes and presents them to the Father
5. Deuteronomy 26:15: "Look down from thy holy habitation, from heaven, and bless thy people Israel, and the land which thou hast given us, as thou swarest unto our fathers, a land that floweth with milk and honey."

**C. Proverbs 3:9-10—Tithing Produces the Overflow**
1. "Honour the Lord with thy substance, and with the firstfruits of all thine increase: So shall thy barns be filled with plenty, and thy presses shall burst out with new wine."
2. AMP: "Honor the Lord with your capital and sufficiency [from righteous labors] and with the firstfruits of all your income; so shall your storage places be filled with plenty, and your vats shall be overflowing with new wine."
3. MSG: "Honor God with everything you own; give him the first and the best. Your barns will burst, and your wine vats will brim over."

## D. A Farmer's Experiment in Tithing
*From a book written in 1940 by a farmer named Perry Hayden*

Perry Hayden heard his pastor preach a message about tithing.

He decided to try an experiment to see how much harvest a seed would produce.

His plan was to sow one cubic inch of wheat—360 kernels. He committed to the Lord that, for a period of six years, he would tithe 10 percent of the harvest and sow the rest.

In the first year, it took a 4-foot by 8-foot plot of land to sow one cubic inch of seed. At harvest time, he scraped the ground in order to get every kernel of wheat. Every precious seed counted. The first year produced a fiftyfold harvest.

He tithed 10 percent.

In the second year, it took 24' x 60' plot of land to sow the seed from the harvest of the first year.

He tithed 10 percent.

In the third year, it took three-quarters of an acre to sow.

He tithed 10 percent.

In the fourth year, it took 14 acres to sow.

He tithed 10 percent.

In the fifth year, it took 230 acres to sow.

He tithed 10 percent.

By the sixth year, it took over 2600 acres to sow 5,000 bushels.

Three hundred sixty kernels had turned into 55 billion. And the largest yield was only fiftyfold. Perry Hayden made $288,000 in six years compared to the other farmers who only made an average of $21,000.

The experiment worked. God can bless your harvest when you tithe.

## EAGLE MOUNTAIN
### INTERNATIONAL CHURCH

## DAYS OF PROSPERITY
**Pastor George Pearsons**

## How to Believe God for a House—Part 1

### Day #46

**A. Romans 13:8 (AMP)—Keep Out of Debt**
1. In 1967, Kenneth and Gloria determined that whatever they saw in God's Word, they would do
2. "If faith won't get it, we won't have it. If the Word won't get it, we don't need it."
3. Then they found Romans 13:8 (AMP) that says, "Keep out of debt and owe no man anything, except to love one another."
4. They committed to live debt free
5. From *God's Will Is Prosperity* by Gloria Copeland
    a. "The first thing I began to believe God for was a home."
    b. "But what about Romans 13:8? It says that we are to owe no man anything but to love him. How can you believe God for enough money to buy a home?
    c. "This is one area most people think impossible."
    d. "Many have made the statement, 'Surely you don't have to believe for a home without borrowing money!'"

**B. 2 Corinthians 9:8 (AMP)—"I hung my faith on that scripture."**
1. "Satan told me that there was no way I could have a home without borrowing money for it."
2. "Believing God was the only way I could have my home."
3. "Satan would come to me with doubt and unbelief, and tell me that there was no way that we could buy a house without going into debt. When he would do that, I would trust in and continually confess 2 Corinthians 9:8 (AMP). It gave me the comfort and strength I needed to stand in faith."
4. "And God is able to make all grace (every favor and earthly blessing) come to you in abundance, so that you may always and under all circumstances and whatever the need be self-sufficient [possessing enough to require no aid or support and furnished in abundance for every good work and charitable donation]."
5. "I hung my faith on that scripture."
    a. "The Word says that He is able to get it to you."
    b. "Don't look to your job."
    c. "Keep your eye single on the Word."
    d. "He is able to get things done."

**C. James 1:5-8—Stay Single-Minded on the Word**
1. "When I believe God for something, I don't waver."
2. "I have made a quality decision that the Word is true."
3. "I have built into myself a reliance on God's Word."
4. "I believe His Word more that I believe what I can see or feel."
5. "As I have heard Kenneth Hagin say, 'If you are determined stand forever, it won't take very long.'"
   a. "That's the way I am when I am believing God for something."
   b. "I could stand forever if necessary."

# DAYS OF PROSPERITY
### Pastor George Pearsons

## How to Believe God for a House—Part 2
### Day #47

**A. Deuteronomy 6:10-11 (AMP)—Houses Full of All Good Things**
1. "We began believing God for the perfect home when we lived in Tulsa, Okla., in 1968."
2. "At the same time, there was a lady in Fort Worth, Texas, who started building her home."
3. "It was several years before I saw that home, but the floor plan was exactly what we needed to meet our needs as a family. It was perfect for us."
4. "She began to build it at the very time we began to believe for it."
5. "God started to work immediately."

**B. Every Step Is a Step of Faith**
1. "We leased the house for one year and agreed to pay cash for it at the end of that year."
2. "We lived well. But as far as having that much money in cash, we just didn't have it. In the natural there was no reason to expect to have it, but in the spirit we knew our God was able."
3. "When we moved in, the house was in need of repair. It needed to be completely remodeled, so I was faced with a decision."
    a. "I had enough money to start the remodeling."
    b. "This is not our house legally. It would be unwise to put thousands of dollars into a house that doesn't even belong to us."
4. "As an act of faith, I went to work."
5. "When Satan would say, 'That sure is a lot of money for you to lose,' I would answer, 'No, in the Name of Jesus. This is my house and it will be paid for in July. We will pay cash for it and I believe I have the money in the Name of Jesus!'"

**C. Galatians 3:13-14—The Revelation of Divine Prosperity**
1. "Our commitment years before to stay out of debt made the difference."
2. "If we had not committed to God's Word then, we would not know what we know today about God's system of finance."

3. "One day as I was standing in my house, looking out the window and thinking about these things, God gave me what I would call a revelation of divine prosperity."
   a. "Divine prosperity works exactly the same way as divine healing."
   b. "We would allow symptoms of lack to come on us and stay there. We were willing to tolerate them."
   c. "I realized that Jesus bore the curse of poverty at the same time He bore the curse of sickness."
4. "You can believe for divine prosperity just as you believe for divine health. Both blessings already belong to you. You should refuse lack just as quickly as you refuse sickness."
5. "If you make up your mind—make a quality decision—that you are not willing to live in lack, but that you are willing to live in divine prosperity and abundance, Satan cannot stop the flow of God's financial blessings."

## DAYS OF PROSPERITY
**Pastor George Pearsons**

## How to Believe God for a House—Part 3

### Day #48

**A. Galatians 3:13-14—The Revelation of Divine Prosperity**
1. Kenneth and Gloria were leasing a house, believing God to buy it at the end of a year
2. The Lord began to give Gloria revelations of how to believe God for her house
3. The first revelation was a revelation of divine prosperity
4. The Lord showed her that she was to stand in faith for her prosperity in the same way that she would stand in faith for her healing
5. "You begin to walk in divine prosperity with a decision to no longer allow Satan to put symptoms of lack on you."

**B. Isaiah 53:5, 48:17-18—The Revelation of Peace and Prosperity**
1. Isaiah 53:5: "The chastisement of our peace was upon him."
2. Isaiah 48:17-18 (AMP): "Thus says the Lord, your Redeemer, the Holy One of Israel: I am the Lord your God, Who teaches you to profit, Who leads you in the way that you should go. Oh, that you had hearkened to My commandments! Then your peace and prosperity would have been like a flowing river, and your righteousness [the holiness and purity of the nation] like the [abundant] waves of the sea."
3. Genesis 15:1, AMP: "Peace and well-being include a prosperous life. God told Abram, 'Fear not, Abram, I am your Shield, your abundant compensation, and your reward shall be exceedingly great.'"
   a. Abundant compensation is far-reaching
   b. Abundant compensation means everything
   c. It enveloped Abraham in a blanket of well-being
4. Peace and prosperity go hand in hand. Your prosperity has already been provided for you. Prosperity is yours
5. *Peace* (HEB) = nothing missing, nothing broken

**C. Genesis 1:26-28—The Revelation of Dominion and Authority**
1. Divine prosperity and abundance belong to you now
2. We, as born-again believers, have the same authority over the earth that Adam had in the Garden of Eden
3. Verse 28 (AMP): "And God blessed them and said to them, Be fruitful, multiply, and fill the earth, and subdue it [using all its vast resources...]."

4. "While we were standing in faith for the money to pay for our house, the Lord reminded me of this scripture and revealed to me that every material thing here came from the earth's vast resources. Every piece of lumber, brick, glass, concrete, mortar—there was nothing in the makeup of our house that had not come from the earth's resources."
    a. "I wasn't taking authority over something that belonged to someone else. That house was up for sale."
    b. "The people had relinquished their authority when they put it on the market."
    c. "I had the right to take authority over it and receive it as mine in the Name of Jesus."
5. "I began to see that I already had authority over that house and authority over the money I needed to purchase it. I said, 'In the Name of Jesus, I take authority over the money I need. I command you to come to me. I take my place and I take dominion over that which I need. I command it to come in Jesus' Name. Ministering spirits, you go and cause it to come.'"

# Just How Far Will You Go on the Word?

## A Partner Letter by Kenneth Copeland

Dear Partner,

Mark 4:20:

And these are they which are sown on good ground; such as hear the word, and receive it, and bring forth fruit, some thirtyfold, some sixty, and some an hundred.

Jesus was teaching on the sower soweth the Word. The object of His teaching was how to produce a hundredfold in this life by using God's Word. Notice in verse 20 it says, "...some thirtyfold, some sixty, and some an hundred." Why did some produce more than others? Were the people who produced a hundredfold better ground than those who only brought forth thirty- or sixtyfold? No. The Word says they were all good ground. We know that God is no respecter of persons, so He didn't just decide to bless one more than the other. They all heard the Word and received it. Something had to make the difference.

We hear people say things like, "Well, you know, these things are just not meant to work for some as well as they do for others." Of course, the person who thinks that way always places himself in the category with those who it does not work as well for.

If we read the rest of Jesus' teaching through verse 32, we find that the seed, or the Word, is what produces. Once we see this, it is obvious that the amount of production is in direct relation to the amount of seed sown. Remember, we are not talking about sowing in bad ground. We have already come past that. We are talking about different levels of production in good ground.

Ask yourself these questions: "Just how far will I go on the Word? Where is my compromise point?" The Word says in Ephesians 6: "Having done all, to stand."

Many people ask me if I believe it is a sin to borrow money. The answer is no. It is no more a sin to go to a banker than to go to a doctor. Of course, there are instances that it would be sin—to borrow knowing you can't pay it back is sin.

When God told Israel that He would make them plenteous in goods and they would lend to many and borrow from none, He meant He would supply them better than if they went to another nation.

The point I want to make is this. When Gloria and I decided to owe no man anything, we made that decision to glorify God and please God by walking by faith. We started by making the quality decision to borrow no more and released our faith to pay all the debts we owed. We were faced with believing for our everyday supply.

We learned to believe for the small things first. As God taught us to prosper, the day came when we knew we were ready to have a home. We were faced with the same question I told you to ask yourself. How far will we go on the Word? We made the decision then that if we ever had a choice, we would use our faith instead of some other source.

It took nearly eight years to get that house by faith. We were in a good enough financial position to have borrowed the money and lived in a better house than the one we were living in all those eight years. Believe me, the faith way was better.

We have the _perfect_ home. It is not just a nice home. It became ours through God working miracles. We began by producing thirtyfold. We grew to sixtyfold. We have grown in this area to a hundredfold on God's Word. Each time before we grew, we were faced with the same question: How far will I go? The Word is strong enough in _any_ situation we are ever faced with to go all the way.

Once the decision is made to increase our capacity for faith and grow in any area, we must then begin to meditate the Word in that area. Give the Holy Spirit the opportunity to teach us and train us in what we need to know in order to produce the hundredfold.

Then came confession. The words of our mouths must continually confess the Word that we are meditating. We must not tolerate any thoughts or actions that do not correspond to what we are meditating and confessing. Having done all to stand, stand therefore, forever if necessary. The growth will come.

You will not only be blessed with the manifestation of what you have believed for, but you will be filled with the joy of knowing your Father is pleased—which is far greater than any physical manifestation of any kind. You hear His voice deep in your spirit saying, "Well done, good and faithful servant."

Jesus Is Lord,

_Kenneth Copeland_

# DAYS OF PROSPERITY
**Pastor George Pearsons**

## How to Believe God for a House—Part 4

### Day #49

**A. Ephesians 6:13-14—The Stand of Faith**
1. "It was six years from the time we started believing God for the perfect home until we moved into the home we live in now."
2. "At the end of the year's lease, we paid cash for our 'faith house.'"
3. "I am still not sure how, except by faith in God's Word."
4. "Had we borrowed the money, we would still have 35 years to pay!"
5. "Thank God, borrowed money is not our source—HE IS!"

**B. This Must Become a Revelation to You**
1. "You cannot receive these things just because I tell you about them."
2. "They must become real to you."
3. "You have to take the scriptures on prosperity and meditate on them until they become a reality in your heart, until you know that prosperity belongs to you."
4. "Once you have a revelation of divine prosperity in your spirit, you won't allow Satan to take it from you."
5. "The Word of God is the source of your prosperity."

**C. Excerpt From a Partner Letter by Kenneth Copeland**
1. Ask yourself: "Just how far will I go on the Word?"
2. "Many people ask me if I believe it is a sin to borrow money. The answer is no. It is no more a sin to go to a banker than to go to a doctor. Of course, there are instances it would be sin—to borrow knowing you can't pay it back is sin. When God told Israel that He would make them plenteous in goods and they would lend to many nations and borrow from none, He meant He would supply them better than if they went to another nation."
3. "When Gloria and I decided to owe no man anything, we made that decision to glorify God and please God by walking by faith. We started by making the quality decision to borrow no more and released our faith to pay all the debts we owed. We were faced with believing for our everyday supply. We learned to believe for the small things first."

4. "As God taught us to prosper, the day came when we knew we were ready to have a home. We were faced with the same question I told you to ask yourself. How far will we go on the Word? We made the decision then if we ever had a choice we would use our faith instead of some other source."

5. "It took the most part of eight years to get that house by faith. We were in a good enough financial position to have borrowed the money and lived in a better house than the one we were living in all of those eight years. Believe me, the faith way was better. We have the perfect home. It is not just a nice home.... The Word is strong enough in any situation."

## D. Seven House Scriptures

1. Proverbs 24:3-4: "Through wisdom is an house builded and by understanding it is established: And by knowledge shall the chambers be filled with all precious and pleasant riches."
2. Proverbs 15:6: "In the house of the righteous is much treasure."
3. 1 Kings 6:38: "The house [was] finished throughout all the parts thereof."
4. Proverbs 12:7: "The house of the righteous shall stand."
5. Proverbs 3:33: "[God] blesseth the habitation of the just."
6. Hebrews 11:10: "[The] builder and maker is God."
7. Ephesians 2:21: "The building [is] fitly framed together."

# EAGLE MOUNTAIN
### INTERNATIONAL CHURCH

## DAYS OF PROSPERITY
**Pastor George Pearsons**

## Jesus—Our Jubilee!

### Day #50

**A. Luke 4:16-21—The Reason Jesus Came, The Message Jesus Preached**
1. Isaiah 61:1-2: "The Spirit of the Lord God is upon me; because the Lord hath anointed me to preach good tidings unto the meek; he hath sent me to bind up the brokenhearted, to proclaim liberty to the captives, and the opening of the prison to them that are bound; to proclaim the acceptable year of the Lord."
2. Various translations
    a. Brenton—the day of recompense
    b. MSG—the year of His grace
    c. AMP—the year for His favor
3. Verse 19 (AMP): "To proclaim the accepted and acceptable year of the Lord [the day when salvation and the free favors of God profusely abound]."

**B. Leviticus 25:9-13—The Acceptable Year of the Lord**
1. The Jubilee was a culmination of all Sabbaths
2. Every seventh day was a Sabbath to the Lord, a day of rest
3. Every seven years, the land was to rest and no planting was to be done
4. After "seven years of Sabbaths," or 49 years, the 50th year was to be the final Sabbath before the whole cycle began again
5. The year of Jubilee began on the Day of Atonement with the sound of the trumpet. During the next year, all property was returned to its original owner, all slaves were set free and all debts were released.
6. No one was excluded because all residents of the land qualified
7. Social status, color, sex or financial position did not matter
8. Every inhabitant of the land could claim back his or her property from 50 years before
9. But the Jubilee of Israel only lasted one year
10. After that, you would have to wait 49 more years for liberation to come around again

**C. Luke 4:21—Jesus Is Our Eternal Jubilee**
1. Verse 21: "This day is this scripture fulfilled in your ears."
    a. CEV: "What you have just heard me read has come true today."

2. The Jubilee became a Person that day—not just a year in time
3. Our Jubilee has come and He is living in us now!
4. We have been liberated from the curse of the law forever—and we don't have to wait 50 years
5. It is time to sound the trumpet of freedom!
    a. We are free from slavery to Satan
    b. We are free from sickness and disease
    c. We are free from fear
    d. We are free from debt, lack and poverty
    e. We are free to receive the fullness of The Blessing